DISCOVERING THE
COUNTRY VINEYARDS OF FRANCE

DISCOVERING THE COUNTRY

VINEYARDS

OF

FRANCE

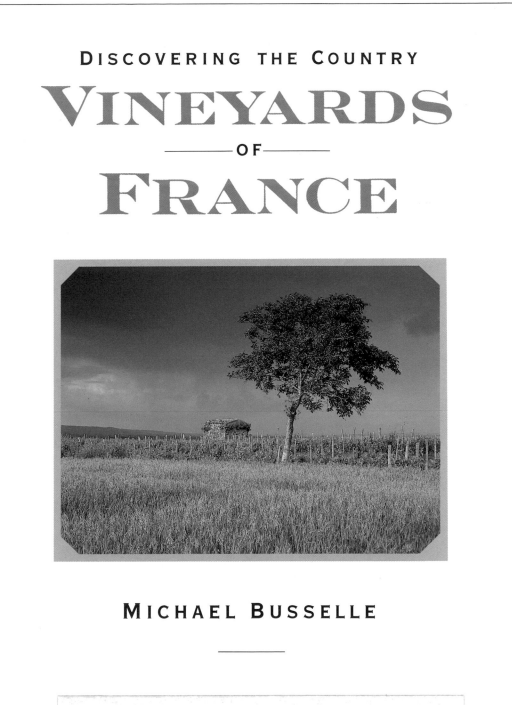

MICHAEL BUSSELLE

Distributed by
Trafalgar Square
North Pomfret, Vermont 05053

PAVILION

FOR PAT

First published in Great Britain in 1994 by
PAVILION BOOKS LIMITED
26 Upper Ground, London SE1 9PD

Text and photographs
copyright © Michael Busselle 1994

Designed by
Andrew Barron & Collis Clements Associates

Maps drawn by Martin Collins

A CIP catalogue record for this book is
available from the British Library

ISBN 1 85145 983 9

Printed and bound in Italy by
Graphicom

2 4 6 8 10 9 7 5 3 1

This book may be ordered by post direct from
the publisher. Please contact the Marketing Department.
But try your bookshop first.

Half-title page: A vine-covered cottage near the village of
Mialet in the *département* of Gard.

Title page: A vineyard of the *cru* of Madargues near
Riom in the Auvergne.

Right: An autumnal vineyard near the village of
Vieillard in the Pays de Bugey.

CONTENTS

INTRODUCTION

Early summer in vineyards near the Pont du Gard.

*I*t's hard to think of a country and a product more closely linked than France and wine. Although we have become accustomed to seeing, and drinking, wines from places like Eastern Europe, Australia, California and South America, the wines of these countries will never have the same, deeply ingrained familiarity as those of France.

It's hardly surprising, for vast areas of France have been devoted to wine production for very many centuries, and their history, culture, and even the landscape itself, shaped by the cultivation of the vine. Even a casual glance at a French road map will reveal a sequence of names which seem more at home on a wine label than a road sign – Vouvray, Sancerre, St Emilion, Chablis, Nuits-St-Georges, Beaumes-de-Venise, Châteauneuf-du-Pape . . . the list seems to be endless, and countless books and articles have been written about these wine-producing locations.

There is another, less familiar, side to the French wine tradition, however, one that has always existed but has tended to be known only by those who live or travel there. It might be described as the wine the French themselves drink casually, at home or in local bars and cafés, but seldom in the grander restaurants singled out by Gault-Millau and Michelin.

Menu du Jour – 50 Francs – Vin Compris! Not such a familiar sign these days, but it can still be seen occasionally in village restaurants and at roadside Relais Routiers. Thirty or more years ago, when I first started travelling to France, such signs were commonplace. In those days it was called Vin Ordinaire, and in many cases the wine was indeed an anonymous table wine, but if you were travelling in wine-growing country it was likely to be a well-made wine from a local *vigneron* who sold some of his production in bulk to his neighbours.

The French wine authorities ANIVIT have taken steps in recent years to identify such wines and provide them with a status and quality control which separates them from ordinary table wines of unknown origins. The establishment of an official Vin de Pays category was made in 1973 with the wines admitted being subject to similar, but less stringent, regulations and tasting panels as the better-known AOC (Appellation d'Origine Contrôlée) wines.

French Vins de Pays have gained enormously in importance during the past two decades. The prices of many of the more prestigious AOC wines have risen dramatically in recent years, and Vins de Pays have gained in acceptability as an affordable alternative. They have also improved enormously in terms of both quality and reliability. As a result, the shelves of wine merchants and supermarkets now contain a wide range of French Vins de Pays from regions, villages and vineyards whose names do not have the same familiarity as those of the AOC wines.

There are now over 140 Vin de Pays appellations, whose definition is a Vin de Table with a defined region of origin. There are three categories of Vin de Pays. A regional appellation can be applied to wines produced in a number of different *départements*, such as Jardin de la France in the Loire region or Comté Tolosan in the Midi. A 'departmental' Vin de Pays, like Hérault, can only be made from vineyards within that specific *département*. A zonal appellation can apply to a much smaller area within a *département*, such as the village of Cucugnan in the Aude or the Coteaux de Coiffy in the Haute-Marne.

These Vin de Pays appellations form the basis of this book, but I also refer to the VDQS (Vin Délimité de Qualité Supérieure) wines which, essentially, represent a half-way house between the status of Vin de Pays and Appellation Contrôlée wines. Most of the VDQS appellations are also clearly defined wine-growing regions which are quite separate from the AOC areas.

Some Vins de Pays are made from vineyards which fall outside the area delimited for AOC wines, and some are made from the grapes of vines which have not reached sufficient maturity, or are too productive, to meet the AOC regulations. It would be a mistake, however, to think of Vins de Pays as simply cheap and cheerful wines whose prime merit is low cost. French wine-makers have, during the past two decades, become increasingly aware of the possibilities afforded by a Vin de Pays appellation and are, in many cases, making Vins de Pays as well as, or in preference to, AOC wines.

Such a decision enables a *vigneron* to use grape varieties and blends not permitted by the AOC restrictions, and in some cases his Vin de Pays is a superior, and more expensive, wine than his AOC wine.

One aspect of my search for Vins de Pays which has given me a great deal of pleasure is to discover how many of France's lost vineyards are being revived, albeit on a small scale, in regions which were devastated by phylloxera and where the wine-making tradition had been abandoned for several generations.

The wines I have mentioned are well-made country wines of good, often excellent quality, but, with some exceptions, generally lacking in the complexity of flavour and bouquet associated with the finer wines of regions like the Côte d'Or and the Médoc.

Because of this I have not attempted to give detailed descriptions of individual wines. It would also not have been very helpful, as most of them are intended to be drunk quite young and the particular wines I was able to taste would either be past their best or no longer available by the time this book is read. Instead, I have provided information on the grape varieties used by the vineyards I have mentioned, in order to give a general indication of the style and character of the wines they make.

EASTERN FRANCE

Opposite: Vineyards of the Allobrogie near St Pierre-de-Soucy in the Savoie. Above: Haymaking near Coiffy-le-Bas in the Haute-Marne.

The Champagne vineyards which encircle the Montagne de Reims are generally considered to be the most northerly in France. But a better claim to this title can be made by the group of *vignerons* based in the small town of Contz-les-Bains, on the left bank of the River Moselle, just a few kilometres from the Luxemburg border. Here the vines are planted on the steep slopes beside the river and along the south-facing hillside of the valley of the little River Altbach, which flows into the Moselle at Contz.

VIN DE MOSELLE

About a dozen producers farm a total of 10 hectares producing Vin de Moselle, which received its VDQS appellation in 1984. The total vineyard area around Contz is more extensive than this, but some of it is owned by Luxemburg *vignerons* and is only in France as a result of border changes. The grapes from these vines are taken over the border to the co-operative at Remerschen, a few kilometres away, and some of the

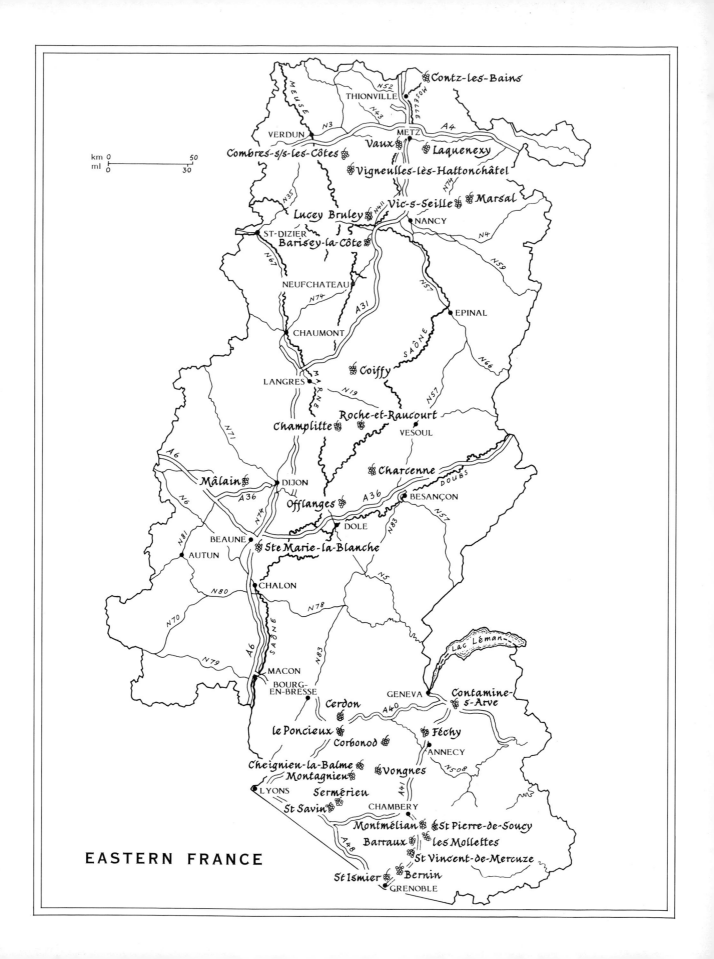

EASTERN FRANCE

smaller Contz wine-growers also have their wine vinified here.

The principal grape varieties grown in the Moselle vineyards are Pinot Noir, Pinot Gris, Pinot Blanc, Auxerrois and Müller-Thurgau. Vin de Moselle is the only delimited French wine using the last variety, which is more commonly associated with German wines, and in fact until 1871 these vineyards were the other side of the German border. However, the Müller-Thurgau vines now found around Contz are largely the result of recent plantings by the French growers.

Joseph Simon, in Contz, is one of these *vignerons*, making an excellent example of a varietal Müller-Thurgau from his single hectare of vines planted on the sharply-angled slope which faces his village house. M. Simon also produces an Auxerrois and a Pinot Blanc, which had just been bottled at the time of my visit in mid April.

M. Simon had just finished planting a plot of Pinot Noir which will be used to produce a red wine and a Vin Gris in a few years' time. He told me that the largest of the Contz vineyards was one of just 3 hectares which belonged to his neighbour M. Mansion at the other end of the steep, narrow Rue du Pressoir.

A few kilometres to the west of Contz-les-Bains is the interesting old village of Rodemack, which has been given the rather optimistic title of the Carcassonne of Lorraine. Named after an ancient Celtic tribe, the Rhoetes, the village was in medieval times the centre of a powerful feudal domain within the county of Luxemburg. It has the ruins of a castle, narrow streets of ancient houses and a fortified gateway, the Port de Sierck, which was reconstructed after partial demolition during the Second World War to allow American tanks to pass through.

A short distance downstream from Contz, on the right bank of the Moselle, the old town of Sierck-les-Bains presents an attractive view of a riverside promenade with an imposing castle set on a hill above.

Vin de Moselle is also produced in the Moselle valley immediately to the south of Metz. The vineyards here were of considerable importance during the Middle Ages, with the income they generated helping to finance the construction of Metz cathedral.

Later, in the nineteenth century, the grapes from the vineyards of Metz were used in the production of Champagne, and the tradition lingers, with many of the Lorraine wine-producers still making sparkling wines in the Champagne style (*méthode champenoise*). The vines now occupy only about 20 hectares in all, but there is considerable enthusiasm among the local wine-growers to continue their regeneration.

One of the leading instigators of the renaissance is the CDEF, an experimental agricultural station near the village of Laquenexy. In addition to 16 hectares of fruit trees planted around the village they also have a plot of 3 hectares of vines on the slopes above Scy-Chazelles, near Metz, on the left bank of the river. In the Middle Ages this vineyard was considered the most prestigious of the region and its terrain the most favoured.

The CDEF produces both fruit and wine on a commercial scale, and the latter has already received considerable recognition, with the 91 Müller-Thurgau receiving a gold medal at the Concours Général in Paris. The range of wines is extraordinary, although quantities of each are understandably small. The current tariff lists varietal wines made from Müller-Thurgau, Auxerrois, Pinot Noir, Pinot Blanc, Pinot Gris, Riesling, Gewürztraminer, Gamay, Muscat, Chardonnay, Sauvignon Blanc, Poulsard and Cabernet. In addition, a white wine is made from a blend of Pinot Blanc and Auxerrois, and a red from Pinot Noir and Gamay.

A few kilometres upstream is the village of Vaux, clustered around a rather faded eighteenth-century château. Here Jean-Marie Diligent and his daughter

Spring flowers blooming between the vines near the village of Contz-les-Bains in the *département* of Moselle.

Marie farm $3\frac{1}{2}$ hectares of vines on the hillside over-looking the valley. M. Diligent grows a small amount of Chardonnay, Pinot Gris and Pinot Blanc, but his principal varieties are Auxerrois, Müller-Thurgau and Pinot Noir. The latter was used to produce a most interesting white wine in 1991, but it is not made every year. The château and its *caveau* are only open to visitors on Saturdays (2–6 p.m.), but on other days the wines can be bought in the village's *épicerie* in the Rue des Mirabelles.

M. Diligent also vinifies the wine of Georges Jaspard in the village of Marieulles-Vezon, making a Vin Gris from a blend of Pinot Noir and Auxerrois and a white wine from the latter alone.

The third pocket of Vin de Moselle vines can be found to the south-east, around the villages of Vic-sur-Seille and Marsal, about 30 kilometres north-east of Nancy. Gris de Vic is a wine with a long history, and Raymond André of Vic was one of the few main producers, with 4 hectares of vines on the hillsides above the hamlet of Vic-Salon. Before his retirement, M. André made only Vin Gris from a blend of Pinot Noir, Auxerrois, Pinot Gris and Gamay, but he sold his vineyard to Jean-Marie Diligent a few years ago. The wine is still called Gris de Vic, and the label, rather touchingly, acknowledges its creator: 'Vignes de M. Raymond André'.

Claude Gauthier at the hamlet of Manhoué, further along the valley of the Seille to the north-west, makes Gris de Vic together with red and rosé from Pinot Noir and white wines from Müller-Thurgau and Auxerrois. MM. Walter and Marchal at Marsal also make white Vin de Moselle from Müller-Thurgau and Auxerrois as well as a rosé from Pinot Noir.

Marsal is a curious village a few kilometres to the east of Vic, dominated by a massive fortified gateway and the remains of ramparts. These were built by Vauban to protect the deposits of salt which made the region wealthy during the Middle Ages. A museum, La Maison du Sel, explains the 4,000-year history of salt extraction and how it is achieved today.

CÔTES DE LA MEUSE

Between the valley of the Moselle and the River Meuse to the west lies the Parc Régional de Lorraine. The river called the Rupt de Mad carves an attractive valley which bisects the region, at the centre of which is the Lac de Madine, one of numerous lakes and pools scattered throughout a pocket of countryside known as the Woëvre.

The plain of the Woëvre is separated from the River Meuse by a range of hills called Les Côtes, the crests of which are densely wooded. On the slopes are large areas of orchard, producing the region's speciality crop, the mirabelle, a small golden plum which is used to make jams, tarts and the local *eau de vie*, Mirabelle de Lorraine. Between the orchards are small plots of vines which produce a wine that is locally renowned, but otherwise almost unheard of, Vin de Pays de la Meuse.

The production area is very small, with a total of just 35 hectares spread between six producers in the villages of Combres-sous-les-Côtes, St Maurice-sous-les-Côtes, Billy-sous-les-Côtes, and Creuë.

Véronique and Jean-Marc Léonard farm 5 hectares of vines at the Domaine de Muzy, near the village of Combres-sous-les-Côtes. Here the Auxerrois variety is the predominant crop, from which they make a varietal white wine. They also make a locally-acclaimed Chardonnay as well as a Vin Gris from Pinot Noir and Gamay – sometimes blended, sometimes separately. These vines are also used to produce small quantities of varietal red wines.

At the nearby village of Billy-sous-les-Côtes, MM. Pierson and Blanpied have 10 hectares of vines making Vin Gris, a red wine from Pinot Noir and a white from a blend of Chardonnay and Auxerrois. Mirabelles are also grown here, with the best fruit going to the local co-operative and the remainder used to make Mirabelle de Lorraine.

The village of Vigneulles-lès-Hattonchâtel lies in the centre of this region, and a shop here called La Ferme Gourmande sells many of the wines from local producers together with a variety of regional products, including Mirabelle de Lorraine, honey, jars of preserved mirabelles, *quetsch* and jams, together with *foie gras*, *confits* and *charcuterie*.

Quiche Lorraine is the region's most famous speciality, but Tourte Lorraine is more popular locally and perhaps more typical. It is a shallow pie filled with minced pork which has been marinated in white wine and cooked with garlic and herbs, with a final addition of beaten eggs and cream introduced through a hole in the crust before it is fully baked.

Opposite: Cherry trees in full bloom in the village of Billy-sous-les-Côtes in the *département* of Meuse.

The old village of Hattonchâtel is set on a hill above Vigneulles, with commanding views over the surrounding countryside. It has a church with a sixteenth-century carved stone altarpiece and a château which was destroyed in 1634 but was reconstructed in medieval style by an American owner in 1927.

Nearby, beside a forest road, is a memorial to Alain-Fournier, the author of the novel *Le Grand Meaulnes*, who was killed in action here during the First World War. This region was the site of many battles, and there is an impressive American memorial in the style of a Greek temple constructed on the Butte de Montsec, a wooded hill overlooking the Lac de Madine.

At Hannonville-sous-les-Côtes a small museum of rural crafts and traditions has been established in a pair of village houses, together with displays showing the region's culture of vines, linen and hemp.

To the west of Les Côtes, beyond the valley of the Meuse, is the Forêt d'Argonne, a beautiful, peaceful region of densely wooded hills. It was once an autonomous county ruled by the bishops of Chalons, Reims and Verdun, and in its centre, set on a ridge, was a Benedictine abbey around which the small village of Beaulieu-en-Argonne developed.

All that remains today is a charming street of old houses decked with flowers and creepers. Inside one is a thirteenth-century *pressoir* constructed of massive wooden beams which was used by the monks to press 300 kilos of grapes at a time. There is an attractive group of traditional houses and farms of the Argonne to be seen in the neighbouring village of Brizeaux.

CÔTES DE TOUL

The ridge of hills which forms Les Côtes continues south beyond the town of Toul, which is set beside the River Ingressin, linking the Moselle and the Meuse. Between the villages of Trondes and Barissey-la-Côte are the vineyards of the Côtes de Toul, which were given VDQS status in 1951.

Vines have been grown here for more than two thousand years. At the end of the nineteenth century there were 17,000 hectares of vines in the *département* of Meurthe-et-Moselle, 2,000 of which were planted on the Côtes de Toul. Today there are only about 100 hectares, with a mere 15 producers making a living from wine production alone.

While Pinot Noir is used here for red wine, and Auxerrois for white, the region's most renowned wine, Vin Gris, is made from Gamay. Vin Gris is produced by pressing the grapes and fermenting the separated juice without contact with the skin, in exactly the same way in which white wine is made. The colour can vary from being almost indistinguishable from a white wine to a deep rosé. Claude Vosgien, in the village of Bulligny, told me that it depends upon the amount of summer sunshine: the less there is, the paler the wine.

My visit in the middle of April was a couple of months before M. Vosgien's new, very pale, Vin Gris was due to be bottled, but he gave me the opportunity to sample it. I commented on the faintest degree of sparkle, and he said it was known as *frétillant*, which translates as wriggling or quivering, and is the mark of a good, young Gris de Toul.

There is a signposted Route du Vin et de la Mirabelle which leads through the principal wine villages, from Barisey-la-Côte in the south to Bulligny, Mont-le-Vignoble and Charmes-la-Côte to Bruley and Lucey in the north, with plenty of opportunities to taste and buy the wines along the way.

The neighbouring and rival villages of Bruley and Lucey harbour the greatest concentration of producers, including Marcel and Michel Laroppe, Pierre Prévôt, and Dominique Goujot at Bruley, and Lièvre frères and Michel Goujot at Lucey.

An opportunity to taste and buy many of these wines, as well as other regional specialities, can be found at the Promotion Centre of the products of the Côtes de Toul in the village of Bruley, where a gourmet's boutique displays a wide range from a group of a dozen or so individual producers, together with a *caveau* and a small museum of viticultural equipment. It is open every day except Monday (2–7 p.m.) from March until December.

COTEAUX DE COIFFY

The River Meuse rises about 100 kilometres to the south of Toul near the spa town of Bourbonne-les-Bains. A few kilometres to the south-west is the small hilltop village of Coiffy-le-Haut. In countryside which is a considerable distance from any familiar wine-growing regions it comes as something of a surprise to discover neatly-planted rows of vines decorating the slopes around the village.

The area has a long wine-growing history. In the

Vineyards near the village of Coiffy-le-Haut in the *département* of Haute-Marne.

1800s there were 300 hectares of vines here, and there have been small family plots of vines since the phylloxera destruction, but the Coteaux de Coiffy appellation, or the Vin de Pays de la Haute-Marne, is a quite recent development.

A vineyard of just 8 hectares was planted in 1983 by a group of four farmers who also raise cattle, maize and wheat, but this has been increased over the years to a total of 20 hectares. The production is mainly white wine from both Auxerrois and Chardonnay, with a smaller quantity of Pinot Noir and Gamay. There is a small *caveau* in the village of Coiffy-le-Haut which is open at weekends, and one of the *vignerons* lives in the last house on the village's single street opposite the church and is happy, when at home, to welcome buyers.

The countryside around Coiffy is delightful, one of those typically French rural backwaters which time seems to have passed by. A drive through the valleys of the Mance, the Petite Amance and the villages of Varennes-sur-Amance, Champigny-sous-Varennes, Laferté-sur-Amance and Vernois-sur-Mance provides an enjoyable hour or so of exploration.

Perhaps the most interesting site of the region is Châtillon-sur-Saône. A partially derelict hill village of considerable antiquity, it has the remains of ramparts and towers, as well as numerous old houses, and is currently being restored.

For those seeking a quiet and characterful place to stay, the Auberge du Moulin de Lachat, near Enfonvelle, is worth investigating. An old mill house set beside a river and surrounded by woods and meadows, it can be found a short distance to the south-west of Châtillon-sur-Saône.

COTEAUX DE CHAMPLITTE

Even in the small Vin de Pays regions the presence of vinous interest is usually marked by the sight of vineyards, but the Coteaux de Champlitte could well qualify as France's most secret vineyards, since they are tucked away on a remote hillside and can be approached only along a small country track.

Champlitte is a town which lies to the south-west of Coiffy, about half-way to Dijon and 20 kilometres north of Gray. It has a number of old houses, a church with a fifteenth-century Gothic tower, and a fifteenth-century château which is now the town hall and also houses a museum of local history and folklore. The town holds the fête of Saint Vincent, the patron saint of *vignerons*, on 22 January, a tradition which has been maintained since its inauguration in 1632.

The main production of the Coteaux de Champlitte, or Vin de Pays de Franche-Comté, is by a group of 12 *vignerons* who farm the 40 hectares of vines which are planted largely on a single well-exposed, east-facing hillside to the west of the town. The winery and *caveau* are in a building in the town centre and are well signposted.

Before phylloxera, the Coteaux de Champlitte was an important vineyard, with over 600 hectares, but the present venture only began in 1975. Mostly Chardonnay and Pinot Noir are grown, with a small quantity of Auxerrois, Gamay and Pinot Gris, and the wines have attracted numerous medals since the first harvest in 1979.

The valley of the River Salon to the east of Champlitte makes a peaceful and attractive detour, and at the village of Leffond, to the north-west, an ancient washhouse and stone bridge create a particularly charming corner.

About 30 kilometres south-west of Champlitte is the delightful village of Bèze, set at the source of its namesake river, which is a tributary of the Saône. Once a dependancy of an abbey founded in the seventh century, it has retained two towers from the building, and a lovely thirteenth-century house overlooks the square. A famous son of the village was Felix Kir, who was the curate there in the early part of the century and later a mayor of Dijon. He was also the inventor of the popular aperitif of Cassis-spiked Aligoté to which he gave his name.

ROCHE-ET-RAUCOURT

Vin de Pays de Franche-Comté is also made in the village of Roche-et-Raucourt, 15 kilometres or so east

Opposite: Wheatfields and vineyards near the village of Roche-et-Raucourt in Franche-Comté.

An early winter's snowfall dusts the vineyards of the Côte d'Or near Beaune.

of Champlitte in the valley of the little River Vannon. Here the Garnéry family farm 8 hectares of vines producing red and rosé wines from Gamay, Pinot Noir and Pinot Gris, together with a white wine from Chardonnay.

Although small family plots have existed in this region for many years, the present vineyard produced its first harvest in 1987. Wheat and maize also form an important part of the farm's production, but cattle are no longer raised, I was told by Madame Garnéry senior, who observed that the younger generation like to have their holidays.

CHARCENNE

The ancient village of Gy lies about 30 kilometres to the south of Roche-et-Raucourt, and a further pocket of vines producing Vin de Pays de Franche-Comté are to be found here, and in neighbouring Charcenne, under the care of Henri Guillaume. He also runs a

large nursery specializing in vine cultivation, and told me that he has supplied plant stock to many of the English vineyards.

There were around 10 hectares in production at the time of my visit, with new plantings in progress. Chardonnay accounts for about half of the vines, with a balance of Pinot Noir and Gamay, together with a small planting of Pinot Gris.

The village of Gy is worth a visit. Once the property of the bishops of Besançon, it has some charming old houses, a fine eighteenth-century church, an ancient fountain and a château with an unusual angular tower.

OFFLANGES

About 30 kilometres south-west of Gy, the hill village of Offlanges looks out over the Forêt de la Serre. The prestigious vineyards of the Côte d'Or are about 60 kilometres to the west, and once the hillsides around Offlanges were just as densely cultivated, with over

500 hectares of vines before the advent of phylloxera.

A few plots of vines for family consumption have always remained, but in 1973 two local farmers M. Lormet and M. Guell, began small commercial vineyards which have now grown to a total of around 8 hectares of Gamay and Chardonnay. It is interesting to note that the favoured grape varieties here, like others of the Vin de Pays de Franche-Comté, are from Burgundy instead of those grown in the vineyards of the Jura, a short distance to the south.

This small community is one of many to be found throughout France which are busy reviving a wine-making tradition which had been lost for several generations.

CÔTE D'OR

While the famous Appellation Contrôlée vineyards of the Côte d'Or, after which the *département* is named, are planted in the countryside around the town of Beaune, there are two small outposts which produce the little-known Vin de Pays de la Côte d'Or.

One is to be found a short distance to the west of Dijon at the village of Mâlain, where steep rounded hillsides are planted with the blackcurrant bushes used to produce the region's other famous liquid product, Crème de Cassis.

Here, in addition to his locally-acclaimed Crème de Cassis, M. Yvon Michéa produces AOC Bourgogne, Chardonnay and Pinot Noir, and Vin de Pays de la Côte d'Or, from a vineyard of about 10 hectares. His Vins de Pays include red and rosé wines, both made from Gamay, and a white from 100% Auxerrois; he also makes a Crémant de Bourgogne.

M. Michéa's *caveau* is open only on Saturdays between March and December, but his wines may be bought at almost any time in the village bar, Le Bon Embuscade.

The village of Ste Marie-la-Blanche lies about 8 kilometres south-east of Beaune. Here a Cave Co-opérative produces Vins de Pays de la Côte d'Or – a varietal rosé from Pinot Noir and a white wine from 100% Auxerrois. AOC Bourgogne, Crémant de Bourgogne, Chablis and Crème de Cassis are also sold here, as well as a wide range of other fruit liqueurs. A number of the wines are also sold *en vrac*, pumped directly from the vat into re-usable containers, ranging from 5 litre capacity up to 30 litres or more, which can be bought at the cave.

BUGEY

To the east of the plain of Bresse and the city of Lyons, in the *département* of Ain, a tight loop in the River Rhône contains a landscape of steep rounded hills, wooded valleys and fast-flowing trout streams called the Pays de Bugey. The capital of the region is the small cathedral town of Belley, which lies just west of the Lac du Bourget.

'A hundred square leagues of English garden' was how Brillat Savarin described the region. Lawyer, philosopher, musician and gourmet, Brillat-Savarin was born in Belley in 1755 and became the mayor of the town during the time of the French Revolution. The region is known today as Le Pays de Brillat-Savarin, and a foundation in his name actively promotes the food and wines of the region.

The wines of Bugey were given VDQS status in 1958, and the vineyards contain one of the largest cross-sections of grape varieties to be found in any French wine-growing region, with Burgundian vines like Pinot Noir, Aligoté and Chardonnay being grown alongside Savoie varieties such as Roussette, Jacquère and Mondeuse. The vineyards date from Roman times and were revived in the Middle Ages by the monasteries.

The 500 or so hectares of vineyards encompassed by the appellation are planted in the countryside around Belley. Scattered between cereal crops, orchards, walnut plantations and meadows dotted with brown and white cows, they support about 150 producers.

The village of Vongnes, a few kilometres to the north of Belley and sheltered by Le Grand Colombier, is the home of three producers, and one of these, the Caveau Bugiste, offers an entertaining audio-visual guide to the history of wine production in the region.

Here six producers have grouped together, farming a total of about 40 hectares around the villages of Vongnes, Ceyzérieu and Flaxieu. They produce varietal white wines from Chardonnay, Aligoté, Roussette and Jacquère, red and rosé wines from Gamay and Pinot Noir, and a red from Mondeuse.

The ancient village of Cheignieu-la-Balme in the north of the region maintains a traditional *cru* of Bugey – Manicle. Here, André Miraillet produces a red Pinot Noir and a Chardonnay together with a small

Overleaf: Vineyards in winter on the slopes below Le Poncieux near Cerdon.

amount of Gamay from 3 hectares of vines planted at the foot of a sheer cliff to the north of the village. I visited M. Miraillet at the end of October, just after the harvest, and his vats were bubbling away merrily in a centuries-old cellar warmed by a wood burning stove.

Another small vineyard is farmed by his uncle, and a newly-planted vineyard to the east of the village, owned by M. Beaulieu (the proprietor of the Pavillon restaurant in Belley), seems set to ensure the continuance of the name and reputation of Manicle. There is also some local talk of another of the original appellations, Arbignieu, being revived.

At the western edge of the Bugey vineyards on the steep hillsides overlooking the Rhône is the village of Montagnieu, another of the traditional *crus* of the region. Here the father and son partnership of Franck and Jean Peillot farm 5 hectares of vines to produce mainly sparkling wines from Chardonnay, Altesse, Pinot Noir and Mondeuse. They also produce a smaller quantity of still wine from Chardonnay and Pinot Noir, together with a 100% Roussette, which is made from a plot of 60-year-old vines. It is labelled as Altesse, the variety's alternative name, because Roussette du Bugey has to contain at least 20% Chardonnay.

CERDON

From Montagnieu, the D 19 leads north-west to Lagnieu and Ambérieu-en-Bugey. About 15 kilometres or so to the north-east of Ambérieu is the small town of Cerdon, which gives its name to another appellation of the Bugey region, Rosé de Cerdon, an unusual wine made from the vines which are grown on the surrounding hillsides. It is a sparkling wine made, in what is described as the ancestral way, from Gamay or Pinot Noir. It is sweetish and very fruity with a relatively low alcohol level of 8 or 9 degrees. Many producers made a *méthode champenoise* wine which is usually much drier. A considerably inferior wine is also made by carbonating still wine, but it is clearly labelled 'Vin Pétillant Gazéifié'. The appellation also allows still wines to be made, mainly from Chardonnay, Gamay and Pinot Noir.

The countryside where Rosé de Cerdon is produced is one of steeply rounded hills between which delightful narrow country lanes thread their way to a succession of peaceful villages such as Le Poncieux,

Jujurieux, Breignes, Mérignat and Vieillard.

In the more southerly vineyards there are two signposted circuits beginning in Belley which encompass the most interesting places and important wine villages. To the east of Vongnes, which has a beautiful eleventh-century church, is an area of marshland called the Marais de Lavours. It has been made into a nature reserve with an extensive boardwalk built on piles (the largest in Europe) constructed to enable visitors to view the wildlife at close quarters.

A few kilometres south of Vongnes is the Lac du Barterend, a secluded and peaceful lake surrounded by wooded hills, and to the north is Culoz, which lies at the foot of Le Grand Colombier. It has a medieval château and a beautiful garden, Le Clos Poncet, which contains a memorial to Gertrude Stein, the American experimental novelist who made the region her home at the beginning of the century. From here a road leads into the Valmorey region and to the summit of Le Grand Colombier, providing sweeping views of the Alps and the lakes of Geneva, Le Bourget and Annecy.

To the south of Vongnes the wine route crosses on to the left bank of the Rhône, from where there is a breath-taking view over the Belley basin from a point near the village of Parves. To the south of Belley the route leads to the villages of Arbigneu, in the valley of the River Furans, and Prémeyzel in the valley of the Gland, two renowned trout streams. Most of the villages and hamlets in the region have large communal bread ovens which are still periodically used for fairs and festivals. They are roofed with large flaked flat stones called *lauzes*, with a façade framed by flights of stone steps and a decorated gable.

A few kilometres south-west of Prémeyzel, in the village of Glandieu, is one of the most spectacular waterfalls in France, where the River Gland drops from a lofty rock shelf for 30 metres or more. The route continues to the north-east to Groslée, Lhuis and Montagnieu, running along a steep ridge overlooking the Rhône, and then to the villages of Seillonez, Benonces, Ordonnaz and Cheignieu-la-Balme, where there is a small wine museum and a house which was once the home of Brillat-Savarin.

BALMES DAUPHINOISES

South-west of the Pays de Bugey, in the *département* of Isère, is a Vin de Pays called Balmes Dauphinoises. It's a very small and localized appellation covering a

Mountain pastures near the wine village of Parves in the Pays de Bugey.

region of which the main town is Bourgoin-Jallieu.

The vineyards are distributed in small parcels totalling about 30 hectares among nine producers in the villages of Sermérieu, Vézeronce, Veyrins, Corbelin, Granieu, Salagreux and St Chef, with the largest concentration around the village of St Savin, where there are two producers.

St Savin is an attractive village at the head of a pretty valley bordered by steep hillsides where meadows, vineyards and fields of maize are shaded by chestnut and walnut trees. Marc Bonnaire, who farms about 6 hectares of vines on the slopes above the village, makes a pure Chardonnay which represents three-quarters of his production and a red wine from 60% Pinot Noir and 40% Gamay. In the neighbouring village of St Chef, Noël Martin specializes in a sparkling wine made by the *méthode champenoise*.

Perhaps the most interesting producer of Vin de Pays des Balmes Dauphinoises is the Domaine Meunier in Sermérieu, a peaceful hamlet of old stone houses out in the countryside a few kilometres to the west of Morestel. The vineyard was started by M. Meunier's grandparents, and now he and his wife manage about 5 hectares of Gamay, Pinot Noir and Chardonnay on the stony slopes at the edge of the village.

The majority of Vins de Pays are made to be drunk quite young, but M. Meunier has a different approach, and the walls of his cellars are stacked four deep and ceiling high with bottles going back ten years or more. He claims that the unique quality of his soil, the vineyard's exposure and the way in which he makes his wines given them an ability to improve with age.

COTEAUX DU GRÉSIVAUDAN

The River Isère carves a winding valley from the high Alps as it flows west towards Montmélian, where it takes a more southerly course towards Grenoble. Here the Massif de la Chartreuse and the Mont de Granier tower above its right bank, with the Chaîne de Belledonne dominating the left. Between Pontcharra and Grenoble, on the steep slopes beneath the sheer rock

Vineyards of the Coteaux du Gresivaudan near St Ismier in the *département* of Savoie.

walls of the Chartreuse, are the vineyards of the Coteaux du Grésivaudan.

There are about 80 hectares of vines in all, with the greatest concentration around the villages of St Ismier and Bernin. Here there are Cave Co-opératives, as there is at Barreaux, further north near Pontcharra. The co-operative at Bernin makes both red and rosé wines from Gamay as well as a Pinot Noir and a white from Jacquère. A red is also made from a local variety called l'Etraire de la Dui and a white from another rather obscure traditional grape, Verdesse.

In the countryside around the village of Bernin there are three independent producers, of whom Daniel Zégna is the largest, with about 5 hectares of vines. He lives only a few hundred metres from the co-operative at Bernin.

In addition to the grape varieties used at the co-operative, M. Zégna also grows a vine called Persan, from which a red wine is produced. M. Zégna told me that it is very astringent and tannic when young and must be kept for at least four years. Like his Etraire

and Pinot Noir, it is kept in oak casks for six or seven months before bottling.

The Etraire variety originated from some vines discovered growing near a spring at the end of the eighteenth century; Verdesse was widely planted in the region but largely abandoned after the Second World War in favour of the more productive Jacquère.

M. Zégna's most favoured vineyard of Pinot Noir is planted near the hamlet of Craponoz, below a cliff where there is an impressive waterfall. Traces of vines planted here by Benedictine monks in the eleventh century have been found, and the wines now produced from this vineyard are called Domaine de Craponoz.

Between Bernin and St Ismier a road leads via the Col du Coq on to the Massif de la Chartreuse, a landscape of wooded slopes, fast-flowing rivers, waterfalls and bare-rock peaks. In the heart of the region is a deep valley crowded by the peaks of the Chamechaude, the Dent de Crolles and the Grand Som, each rising to over 2,000 metres. Here, near the village of St Pierre-de-Chartreuse, is the monastery of La Grande

Chartreuse, famed for its liqueur as much as for its religious order. The ruins of the original distillery, built in 1860 and destroyed by a landslide in 1935, can still be seen. The secret concoction is now made in Voiron, about 20 kilometres to the west.

From St Pierre the D 512 leads south via the Col de Porte to Grenoble or north through the Entremont valley to St Pierre-d'Entremont and Entremont-le-Vieux. Amid magnificent scenery the road continues to the Col du Granier, from which there are breath-taking views of the Isère valley and the Chaîne de Belledonne as the road descends into Chambéry.

ALLOBROGIE

To the west of Chambéry the River Isère flows through a very beautiful valley from its source in the high Alps. On its northern slopes are some of the most prestigious of the Savoie vineyards around the villages of Chignin, Cruet, St Pierre-d'Albigny and Fréterive, where vines seem to cover every inch of the tillable land. On the southern slopes of the valley, among fields of maize, walnut trees, orchards and pastures, are much smaller plantations of vines, from which are produced the Vin de Pays d'Allobrogie.

You can follow a quite spectacular scenic route through this region by taking the D 923 northwards from Pontcharra and, at Les Molettes, heading north-east along the D 29 to the villages of St Pierre-de-Soucy, Villard-d'Héry and Châteauneuf. It is a region of immense charm and tranquillity, with stunning views to the north across the valley of the Isère to the mountains behind. To the west the great granite mass of Mont Granier dominates the scene.

The Vins de Savoie were elevated to the status of Appellation Contrôlée from VDQS in 1973, and at the same time the Vin de Pays d'Allobrogie was created to allow the vineyards outside the delimited areas to produce less expensive, quality-controlled wines with a local identity. In 1991 a total of 79 hectares of vines producing Vin de Pays were recorded, of which 59 were within the *département* of Savoie.

The wines are primarily white, with the Jacquère being the principal, and most characteristic, variety. But Chardonnay, Chasselas and Mollette are also grown, as well as Gamay for red and rosé wines. There are a total of 21 individual producers in the Savoie, most of whom have vineyards within the small pocket of countryside I have described.

Vin de Pays is also produced at the Caves Co-opératives of Montmélian, Cruet and St André-les-Marches as well as in the *département* of Ain, around Corbonod – on the opposite side of the Rhône to Seyssel. There are two independent producers as well in the *département* of Haute Savoie at Contamine-sur-Arve and Féchy, near Cruseilles.

I visited Phillipe Chevrier near Les Mollettes, who has a relatively new vineyard of just 4 hectares. He makes varietal white wines from Chardonnay, Altesse and Jacquère, as well as a small quantity of red from a blend of Merlot and Cabernet Franc. It was the end of October and, sadly, he did not have a single bottle left from last year's harvest for me to try. He told me that about 65% of his wine was sold directly to the public and the remainder to local restaurants.

At EARL Beauregard, in a big old farmhouse near the village of St Pierre-de-Soucy, Pierre Dufayard has a more traditional approach, making only Jacquère from his 2 hectares of vines. He sells some of his pressed juice to the co-operative in Montemélian, but produces about 13,000 bottles on average each year with his own label. The harvest had just finished when I visited in October and the new wine was bubbling away merrily in the vats to be ready for bottling during December. M. Dufayard gave me the opportunity to taste last year's wine alongside the newly pressed juice and the partially fermented wine, with a handful of his own fresh walnuts, the farm's other main crop, to accompany them.

Of the Allobrogie wines I was able to taste, one of those I liked most was from a small vineyard near the hamlet of Féchy in the Haute Savoie, about 20 kilometres south of Geneva. The village is situated just to the south of Cruseilles on the steep slope of the Usses valley, in sight of the impressive Ponts de la Caille which span it.

Before phylloxera there were nearly 100 hectares of vines planted around the village, but thereafter, apart from a few family plots, there were no vineyards here until 1976, when Jean-François Humbert planted 3 hectares of vines. His white wines consist of a pure Chardonnay and another with 90% Chasselas and 10% Chardonnay, while a red is produced from a blend of 70% Gamay and 30% Pinot Noir. This is just one more example of how many of the lost wine regions of France are gradually being restored, often owing to the effort and enthusiasm of one or two people.

WESTERN FRANCE

Opposite: Beside the Loire near Mareau-aux-Prés. Above: Vineyards near Archiac.

The Loire, at 990 kilometres, is France's longest river. Rising in the mountains of the Cevennes less than 160 kilometres from the Mediterranean, it flows southwards at first before turning on to a north-easterly course towards the Atlantic. Between Orléans and its estuary at St Nazaire it was an important commercial thoroughfare for more than three thousand years.

ORLÉANNAIS

A short distance to the south of Orléans is the source of France's shortest river, the Loiret, which after just a few kilometres joins the Loire at St-Hilaire-St-Mesmin. Within this small pocket of countryside are the vineyards of the VDQS appellation, Vins d'Orléannais, which are planted around the hamlets of Les Muids, Fleury, La Grance, Le Buisson and Le Bréau, with the village of Mareau-aux-Prés the principal wine village of the region.

Vines have been cultivated here for more than two thousand years, and the wines were appreciated by

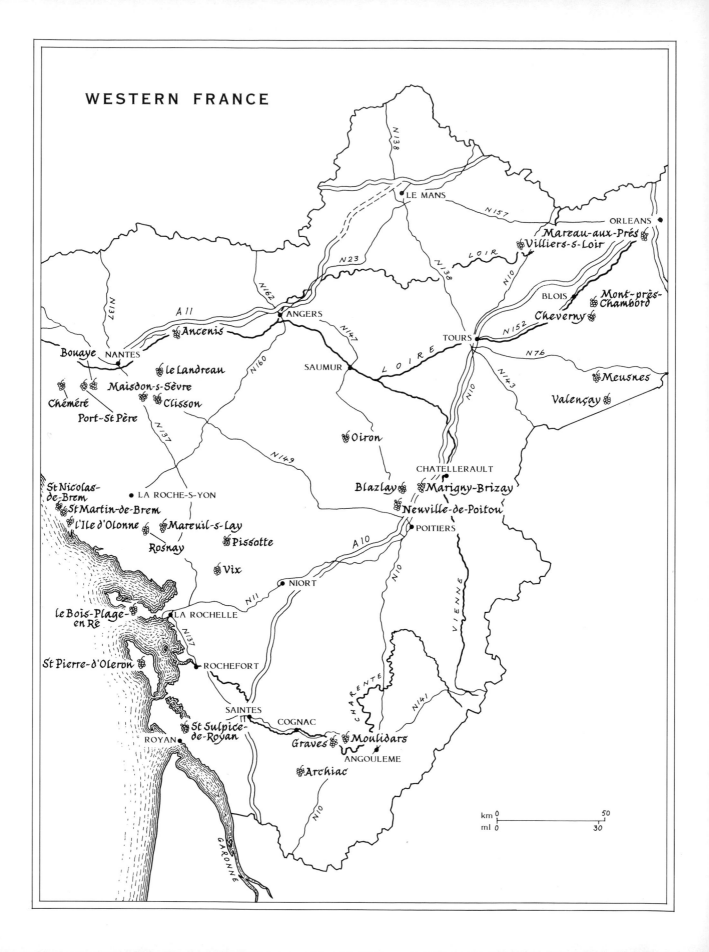

WESTERN FRANCE

Charlemagne, Louis XI and François I, who ordered part of the forest of Orléans to be cleared in order to extend the vineyards. Today they are of a much more modest extent, about 160 hectares, and there are only a handful of producers.

The principal grape varieties here are Cabernet, Gamay, Gris Meunier, Pinot Noir and Chardonnay. The last two are known locally as Auvernat Noir and Auvernat Blanc.

The Clos St Fiacre is a small *domaine* in the village of Mareau-aux-Prés, where the Montigny family farm about 20 hectares of vines producing red wines from Gris Meunier and Auvernat Noir, red and rosé from Cabernet, and white from Auvernat Blanc. Vin de Pays with the regional appellation of Jardin de la France is also produced from Gamay and Sauvignon Blanc.

There is a Cave Co-opérative near the village and another in the town of Olivet, almost a suburb of Orléans. Other independent producers include Lucien Harnois at Cléry St-André, Arnold Javoie et Fils at Mézières-lez-Cléry, and Jacky Legroux at Mareau-aux-Prés.

From the village of Cléry St-André a small road leads eastwards through the hamlets of Le Trepoix and Les Groisons to St-Hilaire-St-Mesmin, closely following the left bank of the Loire with constantly pleasing views of the river and some good picnic spots on the water's edge.

The vineyards of the Orléannais lie on the edge of the region called the Sologne, a mysterious landscape of heathland, forest and silent pools which has been a preserve of hunters for centuries. The countryside of the Sologne looks its best in the early autumn, when the heather is in bloom.

The pretty village of Jouey-le-Potier, 10 kilometres or so to the south of Mareau-aux-Prés, is typical of the region with a collection of old half-timbered houses and a number of ancient pottery kilns to be seen in the surrounding countryside. The old quarter of the market town of La Ferté-St-Aubin, a short distance to the south-east, has some nice old houses grouped around a château built in the style of Louis XIII.

CHEVERNY

On the western edge of the Sologne region is the village of Cheverny, which possesses one of the most striking châteaux of the Loire. Built in the classical style with brilliant white stone, it was completed in 1634 by Hurault de Cheverny and has remained in the same family ever since. Cheverny is also known for its VDQS wines, which are produced from 23 communes on the left bank of the Loire between Muides in the north and Sambin in the south. The principal grape varieties are the Gamay, Cot, Pinot Noir, Sauvignon Blanc, Menu Pineau – known locally as Arbois – Pineau d'Aunis, a variety which is used mainly for making rosé, and Romorantin, used extensively for white wines. This variety is so named because it was introduced into the region when François I brought 80,000 vines from Beaune in Burgundy and planted them around the town of Romorantin-Lanthenay.

There is a Cave Co-opérative in the neighbouring village of Mont-près-Chambord on the edge of the Forêt de Chambord. A red wine is produced here from Gamay, varietal whites from both Sauvignon Blanc and Romorantin, and a rosé from Pineau d'Aunis.

Of the many independent producers in the area, I visited Patrice Hahusseau in the village of Muides on the banks of the Loire. Here he produces a Cheverny Blanc from Sauvignon, red and rosé wines from Pineau d'Aunis, as well as varietal reds from Cabernet, Pinot Noir and Gamay.

Other important producers of Cheverny include the Caves Bellier at Vineuil, M. François Cazan and Philippe Tessier in Cheverny, Michel Contour near Celettes, the Domaine des Huards and Desoucheries at Cour-Cheverny, M. Francis Huguet at St Claude-de-Diray, the Domaine du Salvard and M. Francis Samin at the Domaine de Gaucher near Fougères-sur-Bièvre and M. Jean Pezier at Candé-sur-Beuvron.

The vineyards of Cheverny envelop a number of other impressive châteaux. Chambord lies in the heart of the forest surrounded by parkland and is, perhaps, the most spectacular of all the Loire châteaux; it is certainly the largest, with no fewer than 440 rooms. Seen at the end of a grand tree-lined avenue, its roofline appears like a forest of turrets, pinnacles and towers and, among numerous other beautiful features, contains a magnificent spiral staircase over 30 metres high.

A short distance to the north-east of Cheverny is the Château de Villesavin, built at the beginning of the sixteenth century by the Lord of Villandry, Jean le Breton, who was in charge of the construction of Chambord. The interior can be visited, and there is a collection of old carriages as well as a large sixteenth-century *pigeonnier* to be seen.

Above: The château of Cheverny in the *département* of Loir-et-Cher. Opposite: The château of Valençay in the *département* of Indre.

A few kilometres south-west of Cheverny is the attractive little Château de Troussay, where the outbuildings contain a collection of old utensils, implements and agricultural tools from the Sologne region. A little further to the south-west is the picturesque village of Fougères-sur-Bièvre, which has a feudal castle dating from the fifteenth century.

About 20 kilometres south-east of Fougères is the fifteenth-century Château de Moulin near the Sologne village of Lassay-sur-Croisne. Built of red brick, the château is surrounded by a moat which is fed from the River Croisne. The interior contains some fine furniture, a beautiful painted ceiling and tapestries from the fifteenth and sixteenth centuries.

VALENÇAY

Due south of Cheverny is another fine château in the hilltop village of Valençay. It was built in the middle of the sixteenth century on the very edge of the hill, from where there are fine views over the valley of the River Nahon. The building is set in the midst of a lovely park which is populated by deer, peacocks and other exotic birds. The château was acquired at the beginning of the nineteenth century by Prince Talleyrand, a bishop under Louis XVI and a leading figure in French politics, who used the château for lavish entertainment. Napoleon, who made him a prince, was among the many famous guests.

There is a lively country market on Thursdays where you find the distinctive pyramid-shaped goats' cheese to which the village gives its name. A festival of wine and cheese is held in Valençay on the Sunday following Ascension. The cheese of neighbouring Selles-sur-Cher is also worth seeking out.

The wines of Valençay have a VDQS appellation which covers 40 communes around the villages of La Vernelle, Lye, Villentrois, Faverolles, Veuil, Luçay-le-Mâle, Poulaines, Parpeçay, Menetou-sur-Nahon,

Varennes-sur-Fouzon, Chabris, Selles-sur-Cher and Fontguenand. The countryside is one of open rolling farmland, with the vineyards, totalling about 750 hectares, scattered throughout in smallish plots, the largest concentration being to the south of Meusnes.

The permitted grape varieties are Gamay, Cot and Pinot Noir for reds; Gamay, Cot, Cabernet and Pineau d'Aunis for rosés; and Sauvignon Blanc, Chardonnay and Menu Pineau – also known as Arbois – for whites.

The region's Cave Co-opérative is situated on the D 956 near the village of Fontguenand and is open every day except Sundays. There are also a number of independent producers. The small village of Meusnes, which has a very attractive eleventh-century church, is the centre for ten of them, and a wine fair is held here each year at Pentecost.

The soil in this region is essentially a flinty clay and this gave rise to another quite different industry during the last century, when Meusnes became the centre for the manufacture of gun flints. There is a unique museum in the village which displays the immense variety of shapes and sizes which were supplied to gunmakers all over the world.

I visited M. Hubert Sinson, whose vineyards are planted around the hamlet of Le Musa, a few kilometres to the south-east of Meusnes. In addition to a traditional red and rosé produced from a blend of the recommended varieties, M. Sinson also makes varietal wines from Sauvignon and Cot. At the time of my visit he was feeling very pleased with himself as the planting of 3 hectares of vines on the slopes below the Château de Valençay had just been completed. These will, in a few years time, be used to produce a Clos de Valençay.

Other producers of note include the Domaine Champieux at Puits-de-Saray, M. Philippe Doucet near Selles-sur-Cher, M. Marc Carré at Faverolles, M. Gerard Toyer at Chamcol, near Selles-sur-Cher, and M. Jacky Près at Meusnes.

The D 15 leads south-west of Valençay through the pretty valley of the Nahon to the village of Vicq-sur-Nahon, where there is an elegant eighteenth-century château, La Moustière, and the Château de Coubloust, which has a curious separate tower. Ten kilometres to the west of Valençay is the village of Luçay-le-Mâle, where there is a fifteenth-century château, the fine old manor house of La Foulquetière and an eleventh-century church. Nearby is the lake of Foulquetière and

the River Modon, known for its trout fishing.

You can make a very pleasing round trip through the vineyards along quiet country lanes by following the CD 22A and the D 128 west of Valençay to the village of Villentrois on the edge of the Forêt de Gatine. There are 50 kilometres of caves here used for mushroom cultivation, a fifteenth-century château and a Roman chapel. From here the D 33 continues north to Lye, in the valley of the Modon, with the sixteenth-century Château de Saray and the Cave de Vaux, from which the stones for the cathedral of Bourges were quarried.

The route leads east from Lye to Fontguenand, which has a manor house with a curious tower, La Drevaudière, and then continues north through the hamlets of Le Musa and Porcherioux to La Vernelle, in the valley of the Fouzon, where you can visit the *fromagerie* of M. Jacquin. On 22 January the fête of Saint Vincent is held at La Vernelle, which incorporates a competition of Vins de Pays. From here the route heads south back towards Valençay through the hamlets of Launay, Lucioux, l'Epinat and Les Jumeaux.

COTEAUX DU VENDÔMOIS

Fifty kilometres or so to the north-west of Cheverny the charming old town of Vendôme sits astride the little River Loir. An ancient stone bridge and a fortified gateway lead into the town, and the ruins of a feudal castle stand impressively on a steep rounded hill behind. There are numerous old houses with turrets, gables and towers, and in the town centre, now pedestrianized, is the sixteenth-century tower of Saint Martin. The abbey church of La Trinité, founded in the eleventh century, has a magnificent Gothic façade and a beautiful bell tower.

The Coteaux du Vendômois is a VDQS appellation which covers the communes of Houssay, Lavardin, Lunay, Mazange, Montoire-sur-le-Loir, Naveil, Thoré-la-Rochette, Villiersfaux and Villiers-sur-Loir. The permitted grape varieties are Chenin and Chardonnay for white wines, Pineau d'Aunis for rosé, and Pineau d'Aunis, Cabernet Franc, Pinot Noir, Gamay and Cot for red.

The village of Villiers-sur-Loir, just a few kilometres north-west of Vendôme, is the location of the region's one and only co-operative where they also produce a Vin de Pays du Jardin de la France from Chardonnay.

Jacques and Annie Noury, in the village of Houssay,

are independent producers who make varietal Vin de Pays from Sauvignon, Chardonnay, Gamay, Cabernet and Grolleau Gris – a variety greatly favoured in the Pays de Retz – in addition to their traditional Côtes du Vendômois. The TGV (high speed train) route had been extended to Vendôme shortly before my visit, and the Nourys had marked the occasion with a special *cuvée* presented in a painted bottle.

Other important producers of Coteaux du Vendômois include Jean Brazilier and M. Colin et Fils at Thoré-la-Rochette, M. Dominique Houdebert near Villiersfaux, Jean Martellière at Montoire-sur-le-Loir, and Claude and Giselle Minier at Lunay.

The stretch of river between Vendôme and Montoire-sur-Loir is very peaceful and unspoiled and can be followed quite closely by road on both banks. The village of Les Roches-l'Evêque has a number of troglodyte houses carved into the tufa rock and the old town of Montoire-sur-le-Loir has a ruined château, several fine old houses and a bridge with pleasing views of the river.

A few kilometres away, on the left bank of the Loir, is the village of Lavardin, with a ruined feudal château set on a hill above. It was the stronghold of the counts of Vendôme in the Middle Ages, but was dismantled by Henri IV during the Wars of Religion.

Downstream from Montoire, on the right bank of the river, is the curious troglodyte village of Trôo. It is set on a steep rounded hill and has a warren of dwellings which have been carved into the rock. Many can be reached only by a zig-zag footpath and series of steps. The homes are much more than simple caves, with gardens, patios and luxurious interiors. At the highest point of the village is a burial mound, from which there are superb views of the Loir valley. Nearby is an ancient well and an eleventh-century church which was a place of pilgrimage during the Middle Ages.

THOUARSAIS

One of the grand sights of the mighty Loire is the Château de Saumur, standing on a knoll above the town. The region is renowned for its AOC wines, which include the Coteaux de Layon, Saumur Champigny, Bonnezeaux and Quarts de Chaume, as well as *méthode champenoise* wines which are produced extensively in the miles of caves which are tunnelled into the hillsides around the town.

Just beyond the southern limits of the Saumur vineyards is one of France's least-known appellations, the VDQS Vins du Thouarsais. The town of Thouars lies about 40 kilometres to the south-west of Saumur and is set on a rocky bluff beside the River Thouet. There is a fine view of the town, its château and its picturesque setting from the Chemin de Panorama, which leads along the river-bank from the D 759 towards Cholet.

The village of Oiron, together with its neighbour Bilazais, about 10 kilometres south-west of Thouars, is the focal point of the vineyards and the home of the appellation's leading producer, Michel Gigon, who farms about 7 hectares. He produces both *sec* and *demi-sec* white wines from Chenin Blanc, a rosé from Cabernet Franc and a Gamay red. M. Gigon also makes *brut* and demi-sec sparkling wines from Chenin Blanc, produced by the *méthode champenoise* in the caves at Saumur.

Oiron is an attractive little village and possesses a fine Renaissance château and a seventeenth-century collegiate church. A dozen kilometres or so to the north of Oiron is the troglodyte village of Tourtenay, where there is an extraordinary subterranean *pigeonnier*.

Even more charming is Richelieu, once described as the finest village in the universe, which lies about 45 kilometres due east of Thouars. In 1621 the village was bought by Armand du Plessis, who a decade later celebrated his elevation to the post of Cardinal de Richelieu by building a grand château and enclosing the village behind walls.

Entered by fortified gateways, it has many fine houses around its perfect central square. The town hall contains a museum of art, documents and objects associated with the Richelieu family and the château. To the south of the village, the large park of the château, which was demolished after the Revolution, is criss-crossed by tree-lined avenues with a number of pavilions and an orangery surviving from its former glorious days.

HAUT-POITOU

About 60 kilometres due south of Richelieu is the city of Poitiers. Once the religious and political capital of Poitou, it remains one of the liveliest and most interesting cities in France, with a wealth of fine buildings, streets and monuments.

In the farmland to the north-west of the city,

scattered among fields of maize, sunflowers and wheat, are the vineyards of Haut-Poitou, which were granted a VDQS appellation in 1976. The vineyards were established by the Gallo-Romans in the end of the third century, and, from the port of La Rochelle, wines of the region became a leading export to places like Hamburg, Amsterdam and London.

The vines are planted on the gently rising slopes, called *groies*, which are covered with a chalky soil. The white grapes, principally Chardonnay and Sauvignon, are grown on the higher terrain where the chalk deposits are thicker, while the black grapes, Gamay and Cabernet, are grown on the lower slopes.

In 1865, before phylloxera, Dr Guyot reported that there were 33,560 hectares of vines in Poitou, but today there are only about 1,000. The little market town of Neuville-de-Poitou is the centre of the region's wine industry and the location of the Cave Co-opérative. It has become one of the most successful in the country, with a very active export market. The co-operative is supported by 450 *vignerons* with 820 hectares of vines, representing about 95% of the total production.

The most prestigious of the co-operative's wines are produced from three individual *domaines*. The Château de Logis has 20 hectares of Chardonnay vines, most of which have at least 15 years of growth. The wine is fermented for up to 15 days at a low temperature and bottled in the spring. It also has 11 hectares of Sauvignon Blanc, with vines of a similar age.

The Château la Fuye has 9 hectares of Cabernet Franc and Cabernet Sauvignon, with some vines exceeding 20 years of growth. The wines are given a traditional long period of fermentation and blended in the proportion of 80% Cabernet Franc and 20% Cabernet Sauvignon. They are bottled after being aged for nine months in oak barrels. A rosé is made from Cabernet with just 'one night' skin contact, and lighter young-drinking reds are also produced from Gamay and Cabernet. *Méthode champenoise* wines are made, together with a Blanc de Blancs Brut, from 100% Chardonnay, and a Brut rosé.

A drive through the vineyards can be made by following the D 990 and D 91 to the pretty village of Blaslay, in the valley of the River Palu, and then heading eastwards along the D 15 to Cheneché and

Opposite: Farmland near the wine village of Marigny-Brizay in Haut-Poitou.

Vendouvre-du-Poitou. From here the D 21 leads to the attractive old village of Marigny-Brizay.

Near here I visited M. Descoux at the Domaine de la Rôtisserie, one of the half-dozen or so independent producers. He farms about 11 hectares of vines, of which a third are Sauvignon Blanc, producing a wine with which he has enjoyed considerable acclaim along with his red Cabernet and Gamay. His *caveau* is situated in a large 200-year-old troglodyte dwelling, complete with a kitchen and chimney, which was once the family home.

Another large network of caves, covering 1 hectare in all, houses the winery at the nearby Château de la Marre, which has a vineyard of about 6 hectares. In addition to varietal wines from Gamay, Cabernet and Sauvignon Blanc, a small quantity of Chenin Blanc is also produced here.

The wines of Anjou and Muscadet dominate the western Loire, those of the former being predominantly red and rosé, and the latter exclusively white. The production of Vin de Pays in the Loire region has become rather blurred by the introduction of the regional appellation, Jardin de la France, which has tended to be used for most of the departmental Vins de Pays and makes the precise origin of a Vin de Pays more difficult to identify.

The recent investment in the marketing, advertising and promotion of Jardin de la France has made this name much more widely known. Many producers feel that they will be able to sell more successfully with this label than with one of the departmental Vin de Pays appellations, many of which have tended to disappear under this blanket name.

An exception is Jean Volerit at St Pierre-à-Champ, who makes Vin de Pays des Deux-Sèvres, consisting of varietal red wines from Merlot and Gamay. A neighbour, M. Lemoine, at the Domaine de la Cachère, also produces a Grolleau Gris with the Deux-Sèvres appellation.

MARCHES DE BRETAGNE

The Loire has only two zonal appellations, and happily these have on the whole not succumbed to this temptation. The Vin de Pays des Marches de Bretagne is produced within the region defined for AOC Muscadet and VDQS Gros Plant. Perhaps the reason for its survival is that it has a strong local appeal. In a region which produces exclusively white wines, Marches de Bretagne gives the producers an opportunity to make red wines, and this many of them do with some enthusiasm, planting at least a few hectares of Gamay, Pinot Noir or Cabernet.

The picturesque little town of Clisson lies in the heart of this region. Set beside the River Maine, it has a wealth of old houses in its narrow streets, a ruined château, a covered market hall and an impressive viaduct spanning the river.

I visited the vineyard of Henri Poiron et Fils near the village of Maisdon-sur-Sèvre, a few kilometres northwest of Clisson. In addition to his acclaimed Muscadet and Gros Plant, M. Poiron also makes an excellent Marches de Bretagne Cabernet Rouge. Nearby, Joseph Bâtard makes a Vin de Pays rosé from Gamay.

A few kilometres north-east of Clisson is Vallet, an important wine village which holds a wine market in March. There is a *Maison du Vin* where you can taste and buy the wines from 40 different producers. A lively country market is held in the church square on Sundays.

Another excellent Cabernet is made by André David at the village of Le Landreau, to the north-west of Vallet on the D 37. Nearby, Guy Charpentier makes both red Cabernet and Gamay Marches de Bretagne. Two other notable producers near Le Landreau are Bernard Gratas, at the Domaine de la Houssais, and Daniel and Denise Gratas, at the Domaine de la Rocherie.

A drive through the vineyards can be made by following the valley of the River Maine, taking the D 59 north-west from Clisson towards the village of Monnières. *En route* there is a superb view of the vineyards from the old mill of La Minnière, set on the summit of a vine-covered hill. The route continues to the wine villages of St Fiacre-sur-Maine and La Haie-Fouassière, where a wine fair is held in September.

A few kilometres to the north-east is the fifteenth-century château of Goulaine. From Basse Goulaine you can drive alongside the Loire to the village of La Varenne and then to Champtoceaux, a very attractive town built on a steep wooded hill overlooking the river. Opposite on the right bank one can see the village of Oudon, with its distinctive tower.

COTEAUX D'ANCENIS

Ten kilometres or so upstream is the old town of Ancenis, which gives its name to the VDQS appel-

The wine village of St Florent-le-Vieil beside the Loire in the *département* of Maine-et-Loire.

lation, Coteaux d'Ancenis. The vineyards are largely on the right bank of the river, extending from Varades to Carquefou, and in a smaller area on the left bank between St Florent-le-Vieil and La Varenne.

The co-operative of Les Vignerons de la Noelle at Ancenis is the main producer, but there are also a number of independents. The co-operative's production of Coteaux d'Ancenis is exclusively Gamay Rouge, from about 350 hectares of vines. It also produces Gros Plant, Muscadet, Anjou Villages and Crémant de Loire.

I visited Jean-Claude Toublanc, an independent producer near the village of St Géréon, who has a beautifully situated vineyard on a steep slope which sweeps down to the Loire with splendid views of the river. A group of three large rocks known as Les Pierre Meslières crowns the summit of the hill. M. Toublenc makes both red and rosé Coteaux d'Ancenis, again from Gamay, in addition to his Muscadet and Gros

Plant. Although Gamay is the grape normally used for red Coteaux d'Ancenis, there are a few exceptions, one of them being the wine made from the Malvoisie variety by M. Jacques Guindon at La Couleuverdière near Ancenis.

PAYS DE RETZ

To the south-west of the city of Nantes is a region called the Pays de Retz. The most westerly wines of the Loire valley itself are those of the VDQS Gros Plant de Pays Nantais, but the vineyards extend right to the Atlantic, and it is in this region that the Vin de Pays de Retz is produced, perhaps one of the least familiar appellations in France.

If the region has one distinctive wine it is the Grolleau Gris, a pale rosé made from a variety which is

Overleaf: Fishing platforms along the shore near Bourgneuf-en-Retz.

rarely encountered elsewhere. Also spelt Groslot, it was first recorded at the beginning of the nineteenth century in the Touraine region. Jancis Robinson, in her excellent book *Vines, Grapes and Wines*, says that it is a high-yielding variety producing ordinary grapes and thin wine, adding that today's wine drinker never knowingly encounters a varietal Grolleau. However, it is alive and well in the Pays de Retz and produces a wine which, although unlikely to excite the connoisseur, can be very refreshing and enjoyable to drink.

At the village of Pont-St-Martin, 10 kilometres or so south-west of Nantes, Gérard Figureau of the Domaine des Eudries makes both Grolleau Gris and Grolleau rosé, as well as a red Cabernet and a rosé from Gamay.

A few kilometres west of Pont-St-Martin is a silent and rather mysterious lake, Le Lac de Grand Lieu. Surrounded by reedy fringes and marshy terrain, it is the haunt of freshwater fishermen who paddle across it in flat-bottomed boats to catch eels, pike, tench and zander. The lake can be approached from the village of Passay, where there is a viewing platform from which to observe the abundant bird life.

The abbey church of St Philbert-de-Grand-Lieu at the southern edge of the lake is one of the oldest in France, founded by monks from the island of Noirmoutier in AD815. It contains the sarcophagus of Saint Philbert, who was born in Gascony at the beginning of the seventh century.

Machecoul, 15 kilometres to the west, was the historic capital of the Pays de Retz. Here stand the ruins of the fourteenth-century castle of Gilles de Retz, who fought alongside Joan of Arc. He later became a notorious criminal and the model for Perrault's character Bluebeard.

At Bourgneuf-en-Retz, near the coast, there is a small museum displaying the history and culture of the Pays de Retz, set in a charming seventeenth-century house. The rather bleak, muddy coastline to the west harbours the oyster beds of the Bay of Bourgneuf; the shoreline is covered feet-deep in old shells, and numerous rickety wooden fishing platforms jut out towards the sea. To the north is Pornic, a pretty fishing port at the head of a deep inlet where sailing boats are moored at the foot of a thirteenth-century castle.

On the way back towards Nantes I visited the vineyard of Gérard Beilvert at the Domaine de la Chapellerie near the village of Chéméré, 15 kilometres east

of Pornic. M. Beilvert produces Grolleau Gris and rosé as well as Gamay and a Cabernet which he sells as Jardin de la France. He has a total of 25 hectares of which 19 are used to produce Vin de Pays.

Other notable producers of Vin de Pays de Retz include Ferdinand Bouin, at the Domaine de Bel Air near St Aignan-de-Grand-Lieu; Daniel Chenas, at the Domaine de Buttay at St Mars-de-Coutais; Louis Gilet, at the Domaine des Cinq Routes near Paulx; the Domaine des Herbauges at Bouaye, and Gérard Padiou, at the Domaine des Pries near St Cyr-en-Retz.

FIEFS VENDÉENS

To the south of Bourgneuf-en-Retz is the Marais de Machecoul, a marshy landscape of reed-fringed dikes, streams and muddy creeks threading their way through moist meadows. Here, between Bourgneuf and the island of Noirmoutier, are the borders of the Vendée and a coastline which is almost completely dedicated to the cultivation of oysters.

At Epoids, to the west of Beauvoir-sur-Mer, is a wide, muddy inlet lined by moored fishing boats around which a fisherman's village has developed, with wooden shacks, rickety jetties and shops which well everything from anglers' tackle to boats and outboard motors. There are places too where you can buy a dozen of the freshest oysters you're ever likely to taste, with a bottle of Pays de Retz or Fiefs Vendéens to wash them down.

Fiefs Vendéens is a VDQS appellation which was granted in 1984 to the vineyards of the Vendée, which, as in many other French wine-growing regions, were much more extensive during the Middle Ages. Planted initially by the Romans, the vineyards were taken under the wing of the many abbeys which were founded during the tenth and eleventh centuries, and this led to the appellation being given the appendage of Fief. Both Rabelais and Cardinal Richelieu were admirers of the Vendée wines, which were at one time given the name of Anciens Fiefs du Cardinal.

Today there are a total of about 340 hectares of vines, farmed by 130 *vignerons* who belong to the Syndicat des Fiefs Vendéens. The vineyards are cultivated in four quite separate areas, each producing wines with a distinctive character. More than 60% of the production is sold directly to the public by the *vignerons*, and although there is no Cave Co-opérative there are numerous chances to taste and buy the wines.

Near the village of L'Île d'Olonne in the *département* of Vendée.

BREM-SUR-MER

The most northerly of the Vendée vineyards are those around the village of Brem-sur-Mer, just south of St Gilles-Croix-de-Vie. Brem-sur-Mer consists, in fact, of two villages, St Martin-de-Brem and St Nicolas-de-Brem, which was burnt by pirates in the ninth century and reconstructed in 1020. The little church of Brem dates from this period and was dedicated to Saint Nicolas, the patron saint of sailors. The vineyards extend around the neighbouring villages of Brétignolles-sur-Mer, Landevieille, L'Île-d'Olonne and Olonne-sur-Mer.

The Domaine de St Nicolas at Brem is one of the leading producers in this region and has an extensive modern winery and *caveau*. Red, white and rosé wines are made here by Patrice Michon and his sons, using Chardonnay, Gamay and Pinot Noir from their vineyards around L'Île-d'Olonne, a nearby village marooned within a curious marshy region of muddy creeks and dikes. Pierre Richard at Brem-sur-Mer is another respected producer who makes a delicate 'Rosé d'une Nuit' in addition to his red and white wines.

From St Martin a road leads along a creek to a gloriously wide sandy beach, backed by dunes, which extends for many miles to the north and south. Access to the beach is also possible from St Nicolas, which is busier and feels more like a resort, in contrast to the quiet fishing hamlet of St Martin.

Further north, at Brétignolles-sur-Mer, a small road loops away from the D 38 and follows the wide sandy beach for several kilometres. One of the finest beaches in this region is at the busy seaside resort of St Jean-de-Monts, 20 kilometres or so to the north, where a wide seaside boulevard runs alongside the seashore.

To the south, along the sand dunes backing the Atlantic ocean, is Les Sables-d'Olonne, an elegant town which was custom-built during the nineteenth century as the Vendée's first seaside resort.

MAREUIL-SUR-LAY

About 50 kilometres east of Les Sables-d'Olonne is the little town of Mareuil-sur-Lay, in an attractive setting beside the River Lay, with a twelfth-century church and the remains of a feudal château completing a charming waterside scene.

The countryside surrounding Mareuil contains the largest section of the Vendée vineyards. They extend to the villages of Bessay, Château-Guibert, Chaille-sous-les-Ormeaux, Le Champ-St-Père, Corpe, La Couture, Dissais, Rosnay, St Florent-des-Bois and Le Tablier.

Mareuil is known primarily for its rosé, but both red and white wines are also made from the principal grape varieties of Chardonnay, Chenin Blanc, Sauvignon Blanc, Cabernet Franc, Cabernet Sauvignon and Gamay.

Having tasted a bottle of Mareuil rosé in a restaurant and thought it exceptionally good, the following day I tracked down the small vineyard of La Cambaudière, near Rosnay, belonging to M. Michel Arnaud. Unfortunately M. Arnaud was not at home, but his elderly mother gave me a guided tour of the winery and a tasting of the new wines recently bottled. She was very excited because on the previous day the vineyard had been awarded two gold medals at the Concours Général in Paris for both their white and rosé wines. The white is produced from a blend of Chardonnay and Chenin Blanc and the rosé from Gamay and Pinot Noir. They also make a red, from Gamay and Cabernet Franc.

There is a small outpost of the Mareuil vineyards to the north-east, around the town of Chantonnay, but these are beyond the boundaries of the VDQS appellation and the wine is sold as Vin de Pays de la Vendée or Jardin de la France. Philippe Orion, at the village of St Philbert-du-Pont-Charrault, is one producer making red, white and rosé wines from similar varieties to those used for Fiefs Vendéens.

VIX

The third small area of Fiefs Vendéens wines can be found around the village of Vix, 30 kilometres or so south-east of Mareuil. There is just one producer, the Domaine de la Chaignée, with a total vineyard area of

Opposite: The vineyards of Fiefs Vendéens near the village of Vix.

about 25 hectares. A white wine is made here with a base of Sauvignon Blanc and some Chardonnay and Chenin Blanc. A rosé is made from a blend of Gamay, Pinot Noir and Cabernet, and a red from Cabernet Franc and Sauvignon. Here a source of great pride is that their wines were chosen by Henri Gault, of Gault-Millau fame, for his daughter's wedding reception.

Vix is at the northern edge of one of the most interesting regions of western France, the Marais Poitevin. It's a fascinating maze of rivers, dikes and tree-shaded canals which thread between meadows and fields of grain and pulses. All this was once sea, the Gulf of Poitou, which was subjected to an extensive programme of land reclamation by five powerful abbeys in the region. The work began with the Canal des Cinq Abbés in 1218, but was not completed until after the end of the Wars of Religion. Between 1607 and 1658 Henri IV employed Dutch engineers to develop the elaborate drainage system which still exists.

The attractive village of Coulon, just west of Niort, is one of the places where boats can be hired to explore the many miles of waterways. The picturesque village of Arcais nearer to Vix, also has a small 'port', with boats for hire, and there is a network of country lanes which runs alongside the canals, enabling the motorist to explore the region.

The Auberge de la Rivière on the banks of the River Vendée, near the village of Velluire, about 5 kilometres north of Vix, offers stylish and comfortable accommodation and excellent food in a tranquil waterside setting.

PISSOTTE

The village of Pissotte, just north of Fontenay-le-Comte, is the location of the fourth and final area of Fief Vendéens vineyards. Here too is just one producer, M. Xavier Coirier, with around 12 hectares of vines. He makes a highly-regarded white wine using a blend of Chardonnay, Melon de Bourgogne (Muscadet) and Chenin Blanc, together with an excellent red and rosé.

A short distance to the north of Pissotte is the Forêt de Mervant, which encircles a large lake. A few kilometres beyond is the charming old village of Vouvant, built at the beginning of the eleventh century on a rocky knoll overlooking the green valley of the River Mère. It has retained parts of its ancient walls,

an old stone bridge, the keep of the feudal castle and a Romanesque church with a beautiful doorway.

The Château de Terre Neuve at Fontenay-le-Comte is also well worth visiting. It was built in the sixteenth century and has a number of outstanding architectural features, including two monumental fireplaces and a magnificent dining hall with a sculpted stone ceiling.

CHARENTE

The Cognac vineyards are the first of any great extent which you encounter after driving south from the Muscadet region in the Loire valley. Considered by many to be the finest of all fortified wines, Cognac evolved because of the trade in salt and wheat which existed in the Charente region during the Middle Ages. In those times a few kegs of wine were often included to fill any space in the holds of ships travelling to London or Amsterdam.

Later, in the seventeenth century, it became the custom to distil the wines, which would be diluted on arrival, so that a greater quantity could be carried in the same space. The Dutch called it *brandewijn*, meaning burnt wine – hence the name brandy. In those times it was a cheap, rough wine, a far cry from the refined and expensive product that we know today.

The finest brandies are made from grapes grown on the chalky hillsides around the town of Cognac, in regions known as Grande Champagne and Petite Champagne, but the vineyards extend over a much wider area to produce the lesser Cognacs, and include the coastal area near La Rochelle together with the Île d'Oléron and the Île de Ré.

In addition to brandy, the Cognac region is also known for its sweetish apéritif, Pineau de Charentes, which is made by adding *eau de vie* to the white and rosé wine made in the region. The grape varieties used for both Cognac and Pineau de Charente include Folle Blanche, Colombard, Ugni Blanc – known here as St Emilion de Charentes – Sauvignon, Semillon and Chenin Blanc. In addition to Cognac and Pineau, the region also supports a large and important Vins de Pays appellation, Charentais, and an increasing number of black-skinned varieties, such as Cabernet Sauvignon, Cabernet Franc and Merlot, are being grown to make red and rosé wines as well as white.

There are several Caves Co-opératives throughout the *départements* of Charente and Charente Maritime, as well as numerous independent producers. Among the leading producers are the Cave Co-opérative of the Château de Didonne at Semussac, M. Jean Aubineau near Malaville, Jacques Brard-Blanchard at Boutiers-St-Trojan, GAEC Coulon at St Gilles, the Domaine de la Battue at Arthenac, the Domaine de la Chauvilliére near Sablonceaux, the Domaine de Poncereau at Epargnes, and the Domaine du Taillant near Virollet.

As a general rule the Vin de Pays vineyards are in the less favoured regions further away from the River Charente and the Cognac hillsides, but I visited one notable exception, Maison Brillet at Les Aireaux, on the banks of the Charente east of Cognac, near the village of Graves.

The Brillet family have owned vineyards here since 1646, with over 60 hectares of vines on the Premiers Crus terrain producing both Petite Champagne and Grande Champagne Cognac as well as white and rosé Pineau de Charente. About 4 hectares are used to produce Vin de Pays Charentais with a red and a rosé made from a blend of Merlot and Cabernet Sauvignon. The white Vin de Pays is made from the same grape varieties as their highly regarded Pineau – Ugni Blanc, Colombard and Folle Blanche.

In the hamlet of Moulidars, a few kilometres to the north-east, is a very different vineyard. Here M. Patrick Mallinger farms just a few hectares of vines and makes only Vin de Pays. He produces an acclaimed rosé from a blend of Cabernet Sauvignon and Merlot, but intends to supplement this soon using grapes from a single hectare of Gamay which he has recently planted. He also makes a white wine from Colombard with a small proportion of Ugni Blanc.

Cognac is a rather drab-looking town, its buildings blackened by a fungus which flourishes on the fumes escaping from the thousands of casks in which the maturing brandy is stored. You can visit the *chais*, which are built along the banks of the Charente in the old part of town, and there is a regional museum which shows how Cognac is made.

A round tour of the region can be made by following the road from Cognac east to the village of St Brice, which has a lovely sixteenth-century château set in a park. Nearby, close to Châtre, are the ruins of the twelfth-century Abbaye de Notre Dame de Châtre, hidden by a wood in an area of meadows. Bourg-sur-Charente is a charming little riverside town with a beautiful twelfth-century church and an imposing

Above: Charentais vineyards near the village of Barbezieux.
Overleaf: Vineyards near the village of Gemozac in Charente Maritime.

château which was built in the sixteenth century. The town of Jarnac, to the east, is considered to be the second home of Cognac, where several important shippers have their bases in riverside warehouses. There are a broad tree-lined avenue and fine public gardens which reach down to the water's edge, as well as the Château de Chabannes.

The village of Bassac, 7 kilometres further upstream, is an attractive cluster of rustic stone cottages and narrow streets with a magnificent twelfth-century Benedictine abbey which has an unusual four-storey bell tower and a fortified church.

From here you can continue, never far from the river, to Châteauneuf-sur-Charente and, a little further upstream, to the charming village of St Simeux set on a hill above a wide bend in the Charente with an old mill and a weir.

From Châteauneuf-sur-Charente you can take a scenic drive along quiet country roads through the vineyards to the wine villages of Bouteville and St Preuil. Nearby, at Lignières, there are a fine Romanesque church and two châteaux. To the south is Barbezieux, the capital of Petite Champagne, with many old houses lining its narrow streets, a fine Romanesque church and a fifteenth-century château.

The route now leads north-west to Archiac, where there is a small co-operative formed by a group of nine *vignerons* who make very good red, white and rosé Vins de Pays, marketed under the name Thalassa.

A short distance to the north, near St Fort sur-le-Né, is one of the region's most impressive dolmens set in the middle of a vineyard. The town of Segonzac, a few kilometres to the north-east, is the centre of the Grande Champagne region. Here the rounded chalky hills patterned by immaculately tended vines seem reminiscent of those on the Montagne de Reims in the Marne, where its prestigious namesake is produced. The journey back to Cognac can be made by following the route via the villages of Gente, Gimeaux and Ars, where there is a twelfth-century church and a Renaissance château.

ÎLE DE RÉ

The charming old port of La Rochelle is the point of access to the Île de Ré, via an impressive toll bridge built in 1988. The island is an important production area for Vin de Pays Charentais as well as Cognac and

exclusively for cyclists and, with many places hiring bikes, this makes a very enjoyable and relaxing way to explore the island especially as there are virtually no hills.

The little town and harbour of St Martin-en-Ré is enchanting, with quayside cafés and shops creating an atmosphere which is a happy blend of fishing-port character and pleasure-port prettiness. Further to the west, the village of Ars-en-Ré, if rather more self-conscious, also has a great deal of charm.

ÎLE D'OLÉRON

To the south, the Île d'Oléron, reached by a long viaduct from Le Chapus, also has extensive vineyards and is an important producer of Vins de Pays with a large Cave Co-opérative at St Pierre-d'Oléron. There are some fine beaches here too, but for me the island does not have quite the same appeal as the Île de Ré.

Back on the mainland, don't miss seeing the nearby village of Brouage, stranded like an island itself in the midst of the marshy hinterland to the south of Rochefort. Completely surrounded by walls and entered by fortified gateways, it was the centre for an important and flourishing export of salt during the Middle Ages. Built originally in the sixteenth century, it became a base for the king's troops during the Wars of Religion, and during the siege of La Rochelle in 1628 the fortifications were strengthened and extended by Cardinal Richelieu.

The oyster-beds of Marennes lie to the south of Brouage around the estuary of the River Seudre. Another interesting village, Mornac-sur-Seudre, is to be found on the left bank near St Sulpice-de-Royan. A cluster of low white-washed cottages with a small port beside a muddy creek, the village somehow has an atmosphere more Mediterranean than Atlantic.

About 20 kilometres south-east of Mornac on the right bank of the Gironde estuary beyond Royan is another curious small village, Talmont. Set on a small promontory, it consists of a single street lined by flower-decked cottages. At the end, set on the edge of a cliff, is the tiny twelfth-century church of Sainte Radegonde. It was from here that many pilgrims used to embark on their sea voyage to the shrine at Santiago de Compostela.

Pineau. The Cave Co-opérative, Les Vignerons de l'Île de Ré, at Le Bois-Plage-en-Ré, has a sound reputation and produces a rosé, a Blanc de Blancs, primarily from Colombard, and a 'Réserve du Gouverneur', a particularly good red made from a blend of Merlot and Cabernet Franc.

It is a delightful island with wide sandy beaches washed by the Atlantic tides and backed by sand dunes. There is an extensive network of small roads kept

Opposite: The harbour of St Martin-en-Ré on the Île de Ré.

SOUTH-WEST FRANCE

Opposite: Vineyards of the Coteaux de Glanes in the *département* of Lot. Above: A goose farm near the village of Loupiac in Gascony.

The wines of the River Dordogne are renowned – Bergerac, Monbazillac, Montravel, Castillon, St Emilion, Pomerol and Fronsac are names that most wine lovers will known, but that of the Coteaux de Glanes is perhaps rather less familiar.

COTEAUX DE GLANES

This small Vin de Pays appellation is centred on the small village of Glanes, high on the *causse* above the left bank of the River Cère, near its confluence with the Dordogne, a few kilometres east of Bretenoux. This hilly country has supported plantations of vines for many generations: in the early seventeenth century it was recorded that the wines of Glanes were greatly appreciated by the lords of the great fortress of Castelnau. But here, as in many of France's lost wine regions, the ravages of phylloxera and two world wars left only a few small plots producing wine for personal consumption.

The present commercial vineyard was founded by

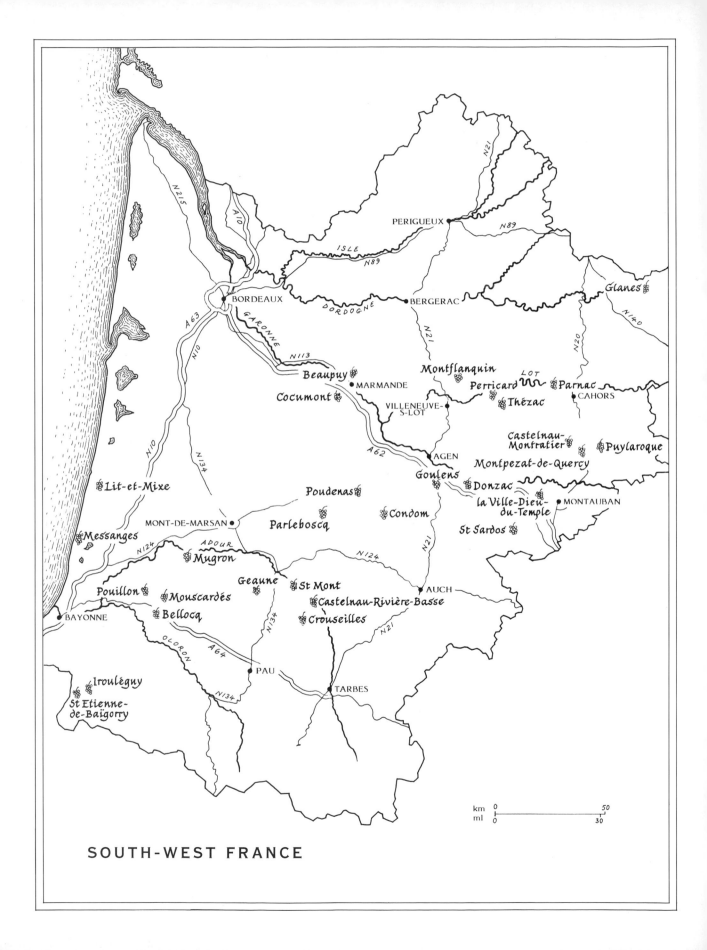

SOUTH-WEST FRANCE

George Vidal in 1976 with a planting of just 6 hectares. At first the wines were known as Vins de Pays du Lot, but a special appellation was created in 1981 which covered an area incorporating a group of six villages. Glanes has remained the centre of production, however, and today there are about 25 hectares which are farmed by a group of eight *vignerons*. They tend their own vines, but the vinification, bottling and marketing are carried out as a joint enterprise in a modern, custom-built winery at the edge of the village.

Red and rosé wines are made from a blend of 45% Gamay, 45% Merlot and 10% Segalin, which is a cross between Jurançon and Portugais Bleu. The grapes are de-stalked and vinified together in stainless steel vats for a period of up to one week, and bottled at the end of April or the beginning of May.

The village occupies a beautiful site on a steep hillside with fine views to the south over the Ségala countryside. The vineyards are scattered in small plantations between orchards of peaches, apples, plums and walnuts. An enjoyable scenic drive through the Ségala can be made by following a winding country lane to the village of Creyssac, to the south-east, then north to Teyssieu and Laval-de-Cère, which lies on the banks of the river.

If any one small area of France could be singled out for having more than its fair share of charming and picturesque villages, then this region would have to be the choice. Ten kilometres or so south-west of Glanes as the crow flies is Autoire, a collection of houses, manors and small châteaux which bristle with towers, turrets, gables and dovecotes. Built of a honey-coloured stone with steeply-pitched roofs covered by earth-brown tiles, many of the houses have small balconies which are reached by flights of stone steps. The village is set in a deep ravine on the north-eastern edge of the Causse de Gramat. At the narrowest part of the ravine, the little River Autoire drops dramatically for more than 30 metres in a series of waterfalls to the valley floor.

A short distance to the north of Autoire is the fortified village of Loubressac, set on the edge of an escarpment overlooking the valley of the Dordogne. It can be seen from a long way off, its ramparts, spires and towers ranged along the ridge like a cockscomb. In the thirteenth century the village was a dependency of the lords of Castelnau but was largely destroyed during the Hundred Years War and rebuilt in the

Above: The Ségala countryside near the village of Glanes.
Overleaf: The fortified village of Loubressac.

fifteenth century. There is a privately owned château dating from this period and also a thirteenth-century church.

The views from the village walls are stunning, east to the valley of the Cère, north to the distant castle of Castelnau and west towards the Cirque de Monvalent on the Dordogne. The small hôtel-restaurant of Lou Cantou shares this view and offers both comfortable accommodation and good food. Nearby, almost hidden by apple orchards and walnut trees, is the picturesque hamlet of St Médard-de-Presque, in a tranquil spot on a hillside overlooking the Bave valley.

To the north-west, the village of Carennac lies along the left bank of the Dordogne in one of its most attractive reaches opposite the Île Barrade, where tall trees shade the water. In medieval times, when the village was a dependency of the abbey of Cluny, a priory and church dedicated to Saint Pierre were built here on the site of a tenth-century chapel. The priory was badly damaged during the Revolution, but a hexagonal tower and a fortified gateway survive, and no one should miss the beautiful carved doorway of the church of Saint Pierre. There are many fine old village houses with gardens which reach down to the water's edge, and the whole place has an atmosphere of great tranquillity and charm.

A short drive to the north-west, surrounded by meadows, the village of Martel thrusts a forest of spires and towers into the skyline. In the centre is a delightful

Discovering the Country Vineyards of France

square with a beautiful timber-framed market hall fenced in by tall, narrow houses. The Hôtel de Raymondie, formerly the law courts and now the town hall, was built originally by the Vicomte de Turenne in the thirteenth century. Nearby is the twelfth-century Maison Fabri, which was the home of Henri Court-Mantel, Richard the Lionheart's brother.

Within a dozen kilometres or so of Martel are three more villages all worthy of a detour. Turenne, to the north, is set on a steep domed hill with the ruins of a castle jutting from its crest, and a few kilometres east of it is the extraordinary village of Collonges-la-Rouge, with houses and manors built of rust-red stone and decorated with towers and turrets, like a collection of miniature castles. South-east from there, the village of Curemonte is strung out along a wooded ridge overlooking the valley of the Soudoire, with three castles, three churches, many fine old houses and ancient stocks beside the timbered market hall. The writer Colette lived here for some years.

COTEAUX DU QUERCY

About 50 kilometres to the south of the River Dordogne, the River Lot runs on a parallel course, and here, held in a tight loop of the river, almost like an island, is the charming old town of Cahors. Once the capital of the ancient kingdom of Quercy, Cahors was the only town of the region to resist successfully the English during the Hundred Years War.

During the Middle Ages the town's wealth was created by trade, banking and wine-making. Vineyards have been here for many centuries, but during the Roman occupation the Emperor Domitian ordered the vines to be uprooted as a punishment for an attempted uprising, and no wine was produced for two centuries. Later, however, the Cahors wines became so popular in England that they were subjected to trade embargoes by the rival Bordeaux wine-shippers.

The most prestigious vineyards lie along a narrow strip of land each side of the Lot between Cahors and the industrial town of Fumel, 70 kilometres or so downstream. There is a signposted wine route which begins in Cahors and leads through the most important villages and vineyards. Before leaving Cahors, however, make sure you see the magnificent Pont Valentré, which spans the Lot. With its three tall towers it is considered to be one of the finest fortified bridges in Europe.

The AOC Cahors wines are exclusively red and made from a blend of Malbec, Merlot and Jurançon grapes. But there is also a Vin de Pays appellation, Coteaux du Quercy, created in 1976, under which white and rosé wines are also produced.

The Vin de Pays vineyards are found principally on the terrain of the *causses* which lie to the south of the River Lot. The region is known as Quercy Blanc because of the silvery stones and outcrops of rock which typify the countryside. The vineyards extend over a wide area totalling over 400 hectares, from the truffle village of Lalbenque in the east to Montaigu-de-Quercy in the west.

In the heart of the Vin de Pays region is the charming village of Castelnau-Montratier, set on a hill overlooking the valley of the Barguelonne. A *bastide*, constructed in the thirteenth century, its name is derived from the fact that it was built by Ratier, a lord of Castelnau, on the site of a previous village which had been destroyed by Simon de Montfort during the Albigensian crusades.

It has an unusual triangular 'square' surrounded by arcades which, on Sundays, is the location of a lively country market with stalls laid out in the shade of plane trees. It was here that I met Mme Dieuzade, whose family farm 6 hectares of vines, planted in 1980, at the Domaine de la Combarade in the countryside to the north of the village.

They make a red wine called 'Tradition', which is a blend of Cabernet Franc, Merlot, Auxerrois and Gamay, and another called 'Clef de St Pierre', which is produced from 60% Merlot, 30% Cabernet Franc and 10% Auxerrois. A 'Rosé d'une Nuit' is made from a blend of Cabernet Franc and Gamay in which skin contact is allowed for just 12 hours or so, creating a very pale and delicately coloured wine. A less expensive red wine, called 'La Rapiette', is also produced from a similar blend of grape varieties.

A short distance to the south-east is the picturesque town of Montpezat-de-Quercy with an arcaded square, many old houses and the fourteenth-century collegiate church of Saint Martin, which contains a number of large Flemish tapestries woven in the sixteenth century.

Near the village on the main road, the N 20, is a

Opposite: The fortress of Castelnau near Bretenoux in the *département* of Lot.

caveau belonging to the Vignerons-de-Quercy, a co-operative formed from 65 individual producers who farm a total of 120 hectares in the surrounding countryside, making red and rosé wines from Cabernet Franc, Merlot, Tannat and Gamay.

About 10 kilometres east of Montpezat-de-Quercy, the little hill village of Puylaroque looks out over the valleys of the Candé and the Lère. A *bastide* built in the twelfth century, it has a number of old houses along its narrow streets, a fine church with a large clocktower, and sweeping views over the surrounding countryside from the village walls.

In the hills to the south, M. Pierre Belon farms 12 hectares of vines at the Domaine d'Ariés. President of the Coteaux du Quercy, he makes a notable rosé from Cabernet Franc as well as a fine oak-aged red wine. Cuvée du Marquis des Vignes, which have won an impressive succession of medals between them.

The Coteaux du Quercy is a very extensive and progressive Vins de Pays appellation with a total of 20 producers, and M. Belon told me the association was pressing for an elevation to VDQS status, which they fully expect to be realized in the near future. The proposal is that the grape varieties grown for the new appellation should be 50% Cabernet Franc, which is known locally as Bouchy or Oeil de Perdrix, and the balance to contain a blend of Auxerrois (Cot), Merlot, Gamay and Tannat, but not more than 20% of any one other variety.

Other notable producers of Coteaux du Quercy include the Domaine de Caille at Labastide-de-Marnhac, Fernand Carles near Puylaroque, Domaine de Lafage at Montpezat-de-Quercy, and the Cave Co-opérative at Parnac on the banks of the Lot.

To aid their cause, the Vin de Pays association staged the first of what will become an annual wine fair on 22 August 1992 at Montpezat-de-Quercy. Here, along with the local wines, such delicacies as roasted wild boar, *cassoulet* and *fondue du tomme* were served, accompanied by ballads, music and minstrels.

There is no official Routes des Vins through the Vin de Pays vineyards and villages, but you can see the best of the countryside by following the signs for the Route de Quercy Blanc and the Route de Chasselas, the dessert grape for which the region is renowned.

Opposite: A hilltop hamlet near Castelnau-Montratier in Quercy Blanc.

The little hill village of Lauzerte, which lies about 20 kilometres due west of Castelnau-Montratier, is one of the prettiest *bastides* in the region, with a picturesque arcaded square. Perhaps the village has been rather over-restored, but it still retains a great deal of charm. It was built by the Comte de Toulouse in 1241, and there are many old timber-framed houses of silvery stone to be seen along the narrow streets which surround the central square. A few kilometres to the north-east is the village of Montcuq, set on a promontory above the valley of the Barguelonette, with the tower of a twelfth-century castle soaring overhead.

LA VILLE-DIEU-DU-TEMPLE

To the south, the River Tarn flows towards its confluence with the Garonne near Moissac. In the centre of the triangle of countryside between rivers is the village of La Ville-Dieu-du-Temple, which gives its name to a small VDQS appellation. As in many French wine regions, the vines were introduced here by the Romans. The terraces on which they were planted were protected by defences constructed by Julius Caesar, for in those times this was the western border of the Narbonnaise Province.

In the ninth century the forest of Agre was cleared by order of the abbots, and the vineyards were extended. Two centuries later the land was given to the Knights Templars, who build the village of La Ville-Dieu. The wines of the Middle Garonne, as they were known, were transported by boat to Bordeaux and exported to England, where they enjoyed considerable popularity. In those times the vines occupied about 1,200 hectares, about half of the tillable land. They were largely destroyed by phylloxera, but with determined efforts the vines were restored and in 1947 the Vin de Ville-Dieu was awarded VDQS status.

The Ville-Dieu vineyards now extend to about 350 hectares and only traditional grape varieties are allowed: Negrette, the Cabernets, Syrah, Gamay and Tannat. The vines are grown in 13 communes around the town of Ville-Dieu, where the Cave Co-opérative, representing over 600 growers, is responsible for the production. The premier wine, red only, is the 'Cuvée Capitouls', which is produced from a blend of 25% each of Gamay, Syrah and Cabernet Franc, with 10% Negrette and 15% Tannat, and is matured in oak for six months before bottling. Two less expensive wines are also produced.

In addition to the VDQS wines, La Ville-Dieu is also the centre for the production of Vin de Pays des Coteaux et Terrasses de Montauban, which was granted an appellation in 1981. Of the total vineyard area about 80 hectares are devoted to the production of Vin de Pays, using a blend of 50% Cabernet and 25% each of Syrah and Gamay.

A Vin de Pays des Coteaux du Quercy is also produced at the co-operative under the label 'Jacques de Brion', from just over 100 hectares of vines planted in the countryside to the north of Caussade. A blend of 40% Cabernet, 30% Gamay, 18% Tannat, 10% Cot and 2% Merlot is used to produce red wine only.

COMTÉ TOLOSAN

Vin de Pays du Comté Tolosan is also produced at La Ville-Dieu. This appellation can apply to a wide area of the Midi-Pyrénées and Acquitaine covering eleven *départements*, and the wine is usually sold in bulk to restaurants and supermarkets. Here, however, it is bottled and labelled 'Armand de Tolose', and is subject to the controls of this specific region, being made from about 30 hectares of vines around La Ville-Dieu. Red varietal wines are produced from Cabernet and Syrah, together with a rosé from a blend of 80% Gamay and 20% Syrah.

ST SARDOS

A short distance to the south of La Ville-Dieu, on the left bank of the Garonne, the village of St Sardos has its own Vins de Pays appellation, with a small co-operative responsible for all the production. The vineyards, in small plots, extend along the hillslopes overlooking the Garonne valley around the villages of St Sardos, Mas Grenier and Verdun-sur-Garonne.

There are about 200 hectares in total, with 150 individual producers. The 'Domaine de Tucayne' produced by a vineyard with 17 hectares of especially favourable terrain, is vinified separately from a blend of Cabernet Franc, Tannat and Syrah and matured in oak casks before bottling. 'Domaine de Cadis' is also a separate production from Syrah and Tannat and is made only from vines with a yield of less than 40 hectolitres per hectare. Two other red wines are produced: 'Gilles de Morban', from Cabernet, Tannat and Syrah (with a rosé from a similar blend of grape varieties), and a basic Vin Rouge de Pays from a mix of Cabernet, Tannat, Syrah, Gamay and Arbouriou.

CÔTES DU BRULHOIS

To the west of La Ville-Dieu-du-Temple, on the left bank of the Garonne, is a region known as the Brulhois, with a VDQS appellation which was granted in 1984. An area of 10,000 hectares distributed over 42 communes is allocated to the Côtes du Brulhois, but only about 200 hectares are actually cultivated at the present time.

Like those of Cahors to the north, the Brulhois wines were once known as black wines for their deep ruby-red colour.

The vines are planted on terraces and slopes overlooking the Garonne, mainly on the left bank but with a smaller area around the village of Puymirol in the hills to the north of the river. The permitted varieties include Tannat, Cabernet Franc, Cabernet Sauvignon and Merlot, together with some Cot and Fer Servadou. The wines are mainly red, but a small quantity of rosé is also produced.

Two Caves Co-opératives are responsible for the majority of production, one near the village of Donzac on the left bank of the Garonne, a few kilometres west of Valence, and the other near the village of Goulens on the N 21 to the south of Agen. Vin de Pays de l'Agenais is also made at the latter.

About 10 kilometres south-east of Donzac is the village of Auvillar, set on a hill overlooking the Garonne. It was one of the many busy ports which developed along the banks of the river and was mentioned in records as early as the ninth century. It was largely destroyed during the Wars of Religion, but was rebuilt and its prosperity restored under the influence of Colbert, Louis XIV's finance minister, who helped to establish factories making writing quills and pottery.

Built almost entirely of red brick, the village has a fine gateway and clocktower, and a beautiful triangular 'square' surrounded by picturesque timber-framed houses and arcades, in the centre of which is a round market hall with a tiled roof supported on elegant stone columns.

To the north-west of Auvillar, beyond the Garonne, the village of Puymirol looks out over the valley of the River Gandaille. A *bastide* built in the twelfth century, it retains a distinctly medieval appearance with many old houses, gateways and a pretty arcaded square. It is also the location of one of the region's finest restaurants, l'Aubergade, where the renowned chef Michel Trama presides over the cuisine.

AGENAIS

The Garonne is one of the most important wine rivers in France. From a source high in the Spanish Pyrenees it flows through a succession of wine regions on its route to the Atlantic; Gaillac, the Frontonnais, La Ville-Dieu-du-Temple, the Côtes du Brulhois, St Sardos, the Agenais, Côtes de Duras, the Marmandais, Sauternes, Entre Deux Mers, Graves and, ultimately, the Médoc, beyond its junction with the Dordogne where it creates the Gironde estuary.

Vin de Pays de l'Agenais is the appellation given to wines produced over a wide area around the old town of Agen on the banks of the Garonne. It extends to the borders of Gascony in the south, to Quercy in the east, to Marmande in the west and to the borders of Périgord in the north.

In practice, however, the vineyards are to be found in three main areas: around the ancient *bastide* of Montflanquin, near Beaupuy and Cocumont in the Marmandais, and near the village of Mézin on the borders of Gascony and the Landes. Apart from a few small independent producers, the production is from four co-operatives based in these areas.

The Caves des Sept Monts at Monflanquin, which is about 17 kilometres north of Villeneuve-sur-Lot, in the northern part of the region, was established in 1967 and, unlike the co-operatives in the Marmandais, produces only Vin de Pays. There are records of the vineyards in the Haut-Agenais dating back to the fourth century, and like those of many French wine-growing regions they reached their peak in the Middle Ages.

The onslaught of phylloxera, two world wars and the changing needs of agriculture almost brought wine-making to an end in this region. However, it is now enjoying a healthy revival, and today the co-operative vinifies and markets the wines produced from a total of about 220 hectares farmed by 200 *vignerons*, for many of whom the vineyard is only a small part of their agriculture.

The principal grape varieties used for the Haut-Agenais wines, which are limited to red and rosé, are Merlot, Cabernet Franc, Cabernet Sauvignon and Cot. A red wine called 'Cuvée des Bastides' is produced from 80% Merlot and 20% Cot; another, called 'Vin de Sept Monts', from a blend of 50% Merlot, 30% Cabernet Franc and 20% Cot.

The superior 'Prince de Monségur' is made from Cabernet Franc and Cabernet Sauvignon and aged in oak casks for up to eight months. A rosé is also made from a similar blend of these two varieties, using the *saignée* method, in which the juice for the rosé wine is bled from the vat during the early stages of fermentation before too much colour has been extracted from the grape skins.

The Cave des Sept Monts is not the only reason to visit Monflanquin, for it is a village of considerable charm. Set on a hill above the valley of the Lède, the village was built in the thirteenth century by Alphonse de Poitiers in the typical *bastide* form of that period. There is a very attractive square, surrounded by covered arcades, and in one corner a fortified Gothic church soars above the rooftops. There is a web of narrow streets to explore as you climb the hill to the square and church, and from a terrace nearby there are splendid views of the surrounding countryside.

A short drive to the north-east leads to a particularly attractive winding stretch of the Lède valley and to the village of Gavaudun, where the keep of a twelfth-century castle stands on an outcrop of rock.

About 10 kilometres to the north is the Château de Biron, a great mass of towers rising from a steep domed hill. It was the home of Charles de Gontaut, who was made a baron by Henry IV in 1598 but beheaded for treason just four years later. The castle roof was extensively damaged in 1972 by a violent hailstorm, but after a period of dereliction the building has been extensively restored and can now be visited.

Monflanquin is one of a trio of *bastides*, and a short distance to the north of Biron is perhaps the most enchanting of them all, Monpazier. Its construction was begun in 1264 on the orders of Edward I, King of England and Duke of Aquitaine, with the aid of the lord of Biron of that time, Pierre de Gontaut. The original grid pattern of the *bastide* construction has been preserved to a remarkable degree and three of its original fortified gateways remain, together with the ancient grain measures in the covered market hall on one side of the square.

If you are at Monpazier it would be a great pity not to visit Montferrand-du-Périgord, just a little further to the north. It's one of the least discovered of the region's many picturesque villages and has retained a quiet, almost hidden ambience. A steep main street rises from the floor of the valley to the ruins of a château set on the summit of the hill from which there are sweeping views of the Couze valley. There are an ancient covered market hall, a church and many old houses, farms and *pigeonniers* hidden among the apple and walnut trees.

Villeréal, 15 kilometres south-west of Monpazier, is the third village in the *bastide* triangle. Like Monflanquin, Villeréal was founded by Alphonse de Poitiers in 1269 but was held by the English during the Hundred Years War. There is a fine fortified church dating from the thirteenth century, as well as a number of old houses and a very attractive covered market hall in the centre of the arcaded square.

THÉZAC-PERRICARD

A short distance to the south-east of Monflanquin is the River Lot, flowing towards its confluence with the Garonne, and just beyond the river, south of Fumel, is one of the forgotten vineyards of France, Thézac-Perricard.

Once upon a time, the story goes, in the reign of Napoleon III, the President of the French Republic, Armand Fallières, entertained Nicholas III, Tsar of Russia, during a state visit. Being a native of the Agenais, and a strong supporter of his local gastronomy, M. Fallières served the wine of the region and the Tsar was so impressed that he placed an order for 1,000 bottles. There was not enough to meet this request and M. Fallières was obliged to tell the Tsar that it was 'sold out'.

The Tsar would probably be luckier today, for the vineyards have been revived and now extend to over 50 hectares, dotted around the countryside in small plots and farmed by 16 individual growers. The output has risen from 25,000 bottles in the first harvest of 1985 to 220,000 bottles in 1990. The vineyards are planted with Merlot and Cot, only red and rosé wines are produced with a base of around 80% Cot.

Thézac-Perricard is in fact two villages about 4 kilometres apart. In 1991 the *vignerons* opened an attractive modern *caveau* near Thézac where you can taste and buy the wines as well as local specialities such as *foie gras* and *pruneaux*. The hamlet of Perricard is a very attractive little cluster of old stone cottages, farm buildings and a small château.

Pruneaux d'Agen are the region's most important harvest crop, and the harvest was in progress at the time of my visit. Laid out in shallow trays inside a large wooden barn, where warm air is wafted by large fans, the fat purple plums are dried to a lesser degree than most prunes and are delicious enough to eat raw, like rich, honeyed candies.

There's a particularly nice place to stay a few kilometres north-east of Thézac near the village of Mauroux. The Hostellerie le Vert, a member of the Logis de France chain, is a lovely old stone manor house set in the middle of unspoiled countryside.

A dozen kilometres or so south-west of Perricard is the ancient hilltop village of Penne d'Agenais. It was a fief of the English kings during the Hundred Years War, but was almost completely destroyed during the Wars of Religion. Although extensively restored, it still has a medieval ambience and there are some interesting old buildings and narrow lanes to explore. Two of the fortified gateways have survived, including the Porte de Ricard, named after Richard the Lionheart who first fortified the village.

A short distance to the south of Penne, in the midst of peaceful countryside, is the tiny fortified village of Frespech, where the château, church and ramparts with their silvery grey stone make a particularly pleasing group.

CÔTES DU MARMANDAIS

Vin de Pays de l'Agenais is also produced in the vineyards of the Côtes du Marmandais, which were promoted to Appellation Contrôlée in 1990. These are mainly to be found around the villages of Beaupuy, just north of Marmande on the right bank of the Garonne, and Cocumont, about 20 kilometres to the south-west on the left bank, which are the locations of the two co-operatives largely responsible for the wine's production.

At Beaupuy both red and rosé Vins de Pays are made from a blend of Cabernet Franc, Cabernet Sauvignon and Merlot, with a period of six to eight days' fermentation and ten months in the vat before bottling. A white wine is also produced, using a blend of 60% Ugni Blanc and 40% Semillon. From a total of 650 hectares about 20% is used to make Vins de Pays. The marketing director of the *cave* told me he was confident that the Agenais Vins de Pays would be elevated to VDQS status within five years because of their excellent quality.

Opposite: The village church of Thézac surrounded by the vineyards of Thézac-Perricard.

At the Cocumont co-operative the production of Vin de Pays is more limited, and only about ten hectares are devoted to its production. Their only wine is a red, made from a blend of Merlot, Cot, Cabernet Franc and Bouchales – a traditional local variety which has been phased out of the Beaupuy production.

In this area you will see large plantations of what appear to be jumbo grape vines but are, in fact, the famous Marmande tomatoes. It seems odd to see them planted like vines, in long orderly rows and trained on stakes and wires.

PAYS D'ALBRET

The other main area of production of Vins de Pays de l'Agenais is to be found about 60 kilometres due south of Marmande in the furthermost corner of the *département* of Lot et Garonne, close to the village of Mézin.

The wine is produced by a small co-operative with a winery established in a small industrial estate at Poudenas, a very pretty village just west of Mézin in the valley of the Gélise. The vines were first planted at the beginning of the last decade, and the first harvest was in 1984 from a total of 25 hectares. Now 21 producers farm a total of around 70 hectares, making exclusively white wine from a blend of Colombard, Gros Manseng and Ugni Blanc.

I first tasted the wine at La Belle Gascogne, a charming hôtel-restaurant set in a sixteenth-century mill house astride the small river. It proved a little more complicated to buy, however, since the winery is used only for production and has no sales facilities. This aspect of the co-operative is handled by Alain Conte, one of the *vignerons* who lives near Mézin. You can find his farmhouse, Le Not, by following the sign to La Ferme de Gagnet from the road which skirts Mézin.

M. Verzéni, the president of the co-operative, told me that they are petitioning for a new Vin de Pays appellation to be created especially for them, since their grape varieties and style of wine are very different from those around Marmande and Monflanquin in the Haut-Agenais. The name would be Vin de Pays d'Albret, since the region was ruled for many centuries by the powerful family of that name.

The village of Poudenas is delightfully picturesque, with a Roman bridge spanning the river by the mill house, a cluster of old stone cottages and a large château set on the hill behind. It was built in the thirteenth century by the lords of Poudenas, who were

fiefs of Edward I, Duke of Aquitaine, to defend the valley of the Gélise, and was further fortified in the sixteenth century. There is an especially fine *pigeonnier* set in a field near the village on the road towards Mézin.

In the nineteenth century the Pays d'Albret was an important centre for the production of bottle corks, and there is a museum in Mézin recording this industry and its history, together with the life of Armand Fallières, President of the French republic between 1906 and 1913, who was born and buried here. His home is near the village of Villeneuve-de-Mézin, where there is a remarkable fortified church dating from the twelfth century.

CÔTES DE GASCOGNE

The Vin de Pays des Côtes de Gascogne is one of the big success stories of French country wines, and much of its success is owed to one Cave Co-opérative, Les Producteurs de Plaimont.

Like the Charente to the north, this region south of the Garonne is best known for its brandy – in this case Armagnac. The success of the Côtes de Gascogne has been particularly important to the region, for the sales of Armagnac, like Cognac, have deteriorated considerably during the past two decades, and the AOC wines of the region, Madiran and Pacherenc de Vic Bilh, have never had a very wide market. The story of the Côtes de Gascogne has much to do with Armagnac and a local grape, Colombard, from which the brandy is traditionally made, and which had never previously been considered by the Gascons as a particularly suitable variety for table wines.

It was the collusion between a local wine producer, André Dubosc, and the renowned chef André Daguin, of the Hôtel de France in Auch, which helped to trigger the rise to fame of the Côtes de Gascogne. During a visit to California they discovered a very good wine was being made there from a variety called French Colombard – a wine which was much appreciated by the Americans. On their return they began to explore the possibilities of a white wine produced from this grape, instead of simply allowing it to be used for distillation.

Les Producteurs de Plaimont, near the village of St Mont to the west of Riscle on the River Adour, were the leading producers of this wine, under the guidance of André Dubosc. Its success was doubtless spurred on by the fact that André Daguin had his own-label version, which was featured on the wine list of the Hôtel de France and sold in the adjoining shop.

The co-operative was formed initially in 1974 by a small group of producers and became a fully-fledged union in 1979 with the aims of restructuring the vineyards, adopting strict quality controls, using modern vinification techniques and expanding their market.

In 1850 the vineyards of the *département* of Gers covered over 150,000 hectares, and today the figure is 25,000, of which the 1,350 Plaimont producers farm a total of 2,260 hectares. This is made up of 790 hectares of Côtes de St Mont, 225 of Madiran, 45 hectares of Pacherenc de Vic Bilh and 1,200 of Côtes de Gascogne.

CÔTES DE ST MONT

The Côtes de St Mont is a VDQS appellation granted in 1957 and incorporates nearly 50 communes around the River Ardour and its tributaries in the cantons of Aignan, Euze, Marciac, Plaisance, Riscle, Montesquiou and Aire-sur-l'Ardour.

At the Plaimont co-operative, red wines are made from a blend of 70% Tannat, 10% Pinenc (or Fer Servadou), 15% Cabernet Sauvignon and 5% Cabernet Franc, and are aged for 8 to 15 months in oak casks. The white wine is produced from a blend of local varieties: 40% Arrufiac, 30% Gros Manseng, 25% Petit Courbu and 5% Petit Manseng. The *saignée* method is used to produce rosé wines from a blend of Tannat and Cabernet.

The Côtes de Gascogne red wines, which form by far the smaller percentage, are made from Tannat with a small proportion of Cabernet. The white wine, called Colombelle, is a blend of 70% Colombard, 20% Ugni Blanc and 10% Listan, but a pure Colombard is also made. Unusually, in Gascony the *primeur* wines are always white, and a Colombelle Primeur is on sale from 1 November.

The majority of the Côtes de St Mont production is by the co-operative, but there are a small number of independent producers, some of whom have broken away from the group. The Côtes de Gascogne, however, is produced over a much wider area and there are many other sources, both co-operatives and independent *vignerons*, in an area north-west of Auch, stretching from Montestruc-sur-Gers in the east to Crouseilles in the west, and as far as Condom in the north.

The riverside village and château of Poudenas in the *département* of Lot-et-Garonne.

CÔTES DU CONDOMOIS

The list of Vin de Pays appellations includes Côtes de Montestruc, a town on the River Gers north of Auch, but the co-operative here has been derelict for many years, and the only local grower producing commercial quantities has opted for the Côtes de Gascogne title on the grounds that it is so much better known.

The other Vin de Pays appellation of the Gers is Côtes du Condomois, and this is widely produced. The grape varieties and style of wine are very similar to Côtes de Gascogne, although the emphasis is more on red and rosé wines, in contrast to the Côtes de Gascogne which is predominantly white.

The co-operative at Condom, for instance, makes a red wine from a blend of 80% Tannat and 10%

each of Merlot and Cabernet, a rosé from Merlot and Cabernet, and a white from Ugni Blanc, Colombard, Gros Manseng and Sauvignon.

Nearby at the Domaine Meste Duran, an independent producer, Patrick Aurin, farms about 60 hectares of vines and makes both Côtes de Gascogne and Côtes du Condomois. The latter is a red wine made from a blend of Merlot, Cabernet Franc and Cabernet Sauvignon, which is matured in casks; the former a white made from Ugni Blanc and Colombard.

There are two other small Vin de Pays appellations in this area. One is Pyrénées-Atlantiques, which is made at the Cave Co-opérative of Crouseilles, just to the south of the village of Madiran. It is sold with the charming name of Vin de Fleur and is a *primeur* made from the same varieties as Madiran – Tannat, Cabernet Franc, Cabernet Sauvignon and Fer Servadou, using grapes from the young vines.

The other minor appellation is Vin de Pays de Bigorre, which is made in small quantities by the Cave Co-opérative at Castelnau-Rivière-Basse, on the D 935 to the south-east of Riscle. Here they produce a white wine from a blend of Colombard, Blanquette (or Mauzac) and Barroque, and a red, sold only *en vrac*, from 50% Tannat and 50% Cabernet Franc.

The countryside of Gascony has a wonderfully open quality, with sweeping rounded hills and a sky which seems limitless. The vineyards mingle with fields of sunflowers and grain, and in the autumn a chequer-board of ripening crops, like millet and maize, make the landscape appear like a sepia-toned photograph.

Condom is a good place to begin a tour of the region. A few kilometres to the west is the enchanting fortified village of Larressingle, a cluster of old stone cottages hidden behind walls, with a fortified gateway, a ruined château and a pretty church. Nearby are the remains of the Château de Beaumont and the hill village of Montréal.

A short distance to the north from Montréal is the very attractive *bastide* of Fourcès, a most unusual place as it is circular, with arcaded houses surrounding a central 'square' shaded by plane trees.

A few kilometres south-east of Condom, near Caussens, is the Château de Mons, surrounded by an experimental vineyard with a *caveau* and winery which can be visited. A little to the south-west is the Château de Cassaigne, dating from the thirteenth century, which was the home of the bishops of Condom. Nearby, the Cistercian Abbaye de Flaran has a beautiful fourteenth-century cloister and an ancient *chai* where wines were once stored.

About 15 kilometres south-east of Condom is the fortified hill village of Terraube, set dramatically on the edge of a hill with its huge castle overlooking the surrounding countryside. Beyond, the old town of Lectoure is encircled by medieval ramparts on a hill above the River Gers. A little further east is St Clar, an attractive *bastide* with the unusual feature of two arcaded squares.

The road south from Lectoure leads through Fleurance and Montestruc to Auch, the largest town of the region with a great Gothic cathedral which is reached from the river-bank by a magnificent flight of stone stairs. Don't miss seeing the prettily sited village of Laverdens, to the north-west of Auch, with a château and church overlooking the valley of the Guzerde.

About 35 kilometres west of Auch is the village of Bassoues, which has a covered market hall straddling one end of the main street and a huge tower at the other. A little to the west the D 102 leads north to the attractive village of Lupiac, set among beautiful rolling hills. The nearby Château de Castelmaure was the birthplace of Charles de Batz, better known as the most famous Gascon of all – d'Artagnan, in *The Three Musketeers*.

Further north, the attractive old town of Eauze holds one of the liveliest markets in the region on Thursdays, with stalls decked with mouth-watering produce set out under the shady plane trees in the church square and adjoining streets.

TURSAN

A short distance to the west of the Côtes de St Mont are the vineyards of Tursan, centred on the little town of Geaune, which is due west of Auch beyond the River Adour. They have existed for very many centuries and were part of the *domaine* of Eleanor of Aquitaine, the wife of Henry II of England. The wines were exported to England as early as the twelfth century, and in later times, between the fifteenth and eighteenth centuries, found markets in Holland and Germany.

The wines of Tursan were given VDQS status in 1958, and today the vineyards extend to about 400 hectares. The majority of production is by the co-operative at Geaune, but there is also a handful of individual producers, including Michel Guérard – the

Above: The fortified hilltop village of Laverdens in Gascony. Overleaf: Place Royale in the village of Labastide-d'Armagnac in the *département* of Landes.

master chef who began the wave of *nouvelle cuisine* and presides over the three-star restaurant, Les Prés d'Eugénie, in neighbouring Eugénie-les-Bains.

White wines are made primarily from the region's special grape variety, the Barroque, with a small proportion of Sauvignon Blanc and Manseng. Reds and rosés are produced from a blend of 90% Cabernet Franc with Sauvignon and Tannat.

TERROIRS LANDAIS

The Tursan vineyards are just within the *département* of Landes, where a Vin de Pays appellation also exists, known generally as Terroirs Landais. There are three distinct areas of production. One is the region to the east of Mont-de-Marsan known as Les Sables Fauves – the wild sands – and here the wines tend to reflect the grape varieties and characteristics of the Côtes de Gascogne.

I visited the prestigious Domaine d'Ognoas, near

Arthez-d'Armagnac, renowned for its fine Armagnac and Floc de Gascogne – an aperitif made by fortifying white wine with *eau de vie*. An excellent Vin de Pays des Terroirs Landais is also made here from Colombard, as well as a small quantity of rosé from 80% Cabernet Franc and Merlot.

A few kilometres to the north, the Domaine de Paguy near the village of Betbezer-d'Armagnac produces a red Vin de Pays from 100% Cabernet Franc. The impressive old château is a *ferme-auberge* listed with the Gîtes organization, and also sells *confits* and *foie gras*.

Just nearby is the village of Labastide-d'Armagnac, one of the prettiest of all the *bastides*. It has a particularly beautiful square, the Place Royale, bordered by ancient houses and stone arches, on which, it is claimed, the Place des Vosges in Paris was modelled (which, before the Revolution, was also called Place Royale). There is a fine fifteenth-century church over-

Landais vineyards near the wine-village of Parleboscq.

looking the square and, in a street nearby, the picturesque Café du Peuple, which is now a private home.

At Parleboscq, a village to the north-west of Eauze, the Domaine de Laballe produces a white wine with a blend of Colombard and Ugni Blanc from 12 hectares of vines. Nearby, at the eighteenth-century Château de Lacaze, the Domaine du Comte produces another outstanding *blanc sec* Vin de Pays from a similar blend of grapes.

COTEAUX DE LA CHALOSSE

The second area of the Terroirs Landais lies to the south-west of Mont de Marsan in a region known as La Chalosse between the Ardour valley and the Gave de Pau, on the edge of the great Landes pine forest. It's a countryside of quiet charm with gentle hills and shallow valleys, where crops and meadows predominate and numerous small areas of vines are planted among them on the slopes.

The region is known for its gastronomy as much as for its wines. Chalosse beef has an Appellation Contrôlée similar to that for Bresse chicken, and the *foie gras, confits* and *magrets* produced here are considered to be among the best in France. Every house and farm seems to have a muddy field with a pond in the centre, and the raucous cackle of geese and ducks echoes through the country lanes.

The major part of the production of Coteaux de la Chalosse is from the Caves Co-opératives at Pouillon, Orthevielle and Mugron – south, south-west and east of Dax respectively. The co-operative at Mugron makes a basic red wine from Cabernet Franc, a rosé from Tannat and a white wine from Barroque.

A superior red wine, called 'Cuvée du Vigneron', is made exclusively from Tannat, with a longer period of maceration giving it the capability to be kept for some

Vineyards of the Landes near the village of Mouscardés.

years. A 'Cuvée du Vigneron Blanc' is also made from a variety unique to the region called Arriloba, which is given a period of eight hours' maceration. This grape is also used to produce a Vin Blanc Moelleux.

There are just two independent wine-makers. I visited the Domaine de Labaigt, where one of them, Dominique Lanot, farms about 6 hectares of vines near the village of Mouscardés, south-east of Pouillon. He makes a white wine from 100% Barroque, a rosé from Cabernet Franc and a red from Cabernet Sauvignon. He told me that his Barroque vines were planted in 1920, and at the time of my visit was busy planting some Colombard in order to supplement his white wine production in the form of a blend. The other independent producer is Jean-Claude Romain at the Domaine du Tastet near Pouillon.

A little to the south of Mouscardés, on the left bank of the Gave de Pau, is the town of Bellocq. At the

Cave Co-opérative here they make a red Vin de Pays des Pyrénées-Atlantiques with a blend of Tannat and Cabernet. This 'departmental' Vin de Pays is also made by the co-operative at Irouléguy in the foothills of the Pyrenees, but is only available *en vrac*.

VIN DE SABLE

To the north-west of the Adour valley is the beginning of the vast forest of the Landes, which stretches away westwards to the Atlantic ocean and north almost to the vineyards of the Médoc, on the left bank of the Gironde estuary. In spite of appearances, the forest is not natural, most of it having been planted during the nineteenth century under Napoleon III.

The industry which developed around the pine plantations has now disappeared, but there is an interesting display of forest life and industry at the Musée de Marquèze, 5 kilometres north-east of Sabres, in the heart of the forest north-west of Mont-de-Marsan. Here, in a forest clearing, a collection of agricultural buildings has been faithfully reconstructed, showing the way of life and activities of foresters during the last century. The museum can only be reached by a train which departs from Sabres.

Vin de Pays des Terroirs Landais is also produced in this unlikely terrain and is called, appropriately enough, Vin de Sable. The main area of production is along the coastal strip between Messanges, north-west of Dax, and St Julien-en-Born, about 35 kilometres further north. Many houses in this region have a small patch of vines nearby for 'consommation familiale'; quite a few have front gardens planted with vines instead of a lawn and flower borders; but there is only a handful of *vignerons* making the wine on a commercial scale.

Madame Thévenin has a small vineyard of about 4 hectares, planted quite literally in the sand at Quartier-Caliot, near the village of Messanges, where she produces a full-bodied red wine from a blend of Cabernet Sauvignon and Tannat. She supplies a number of restaurants in the region, including the atmospheric Auberge des Pins at Sabres, and also sells direct to the public, but only in cases of twelve bottles.

Mme Thévenin told me that she was one of only three 'official' producers of Vin de Sable. The second, the Domaine de Tutet, can be found about 4 kilometres south of the village of Lit-et-Mixe on the D 652. Here Jean Biron makes red and rosé Vin de Sable from a small vineyard of Cabernet Franc and Cabernet Sauvignon, planted in the 1970s. When his roadside *caveau* is closed, M. Biron's wines can be bought in the small shop called Le Tire de Bouchon in the village. The third is the Domaine Point du Jour, on the outskirts of Lit-et-Mixe, where M. Subsol's Vin de Sable can be bought in the village *charcuterie*.

A few kilometres south-east of St Julien-en-Borne is the village of Lévignacq, with an attractive group of traditional Landais timber-framed houses and a fortified church built in the fourteenth century. From both Lit-et-Mixe and St Julien-en-Borne there is access to the vast Atlantic beaches at Cap-de-l'Homy and Contis-Plage, and a little further to the north is the large resort of Mimizan-Plage.

Opposite: The pine forest of the Landes near the village of Lit-et-Mixe.

CENTRAL FRANCE

Opposite: Vines and cherry trees near St Bris-le-Vineux.
Above: A cottage in the hamlet of Villemoison.

Of the vineyards which lie along the banks of the Loire, those of Sancerre and Pouilly-Fumé have become the most widely known and appreciated. They originate from a pocket of countryside scarcely more than 15 kilometres in diameter to the north of Nevers – near the very centre of France. Here the vines are densely cultivated and the hillsides are striped with vineyards as far as the eye can see. These are not the only wines of the region, however.

COTEAUX DU GIENNOIS

The Coteaux du Giennois is a VDQS appellation which applies to a small wine-growing region of about 100 hectares in the Loire valley slightly north of Sancerre, between Cosne-sur-Loire and Gien, about 40 kilometres downstream. Although there are small plantations of vines on both sides of the river along this reach, the largest concentration is to be found on the right bank to the east of Cosne-sur-Loire, around the villages of Cours, St Loup, St Père and Pougny.

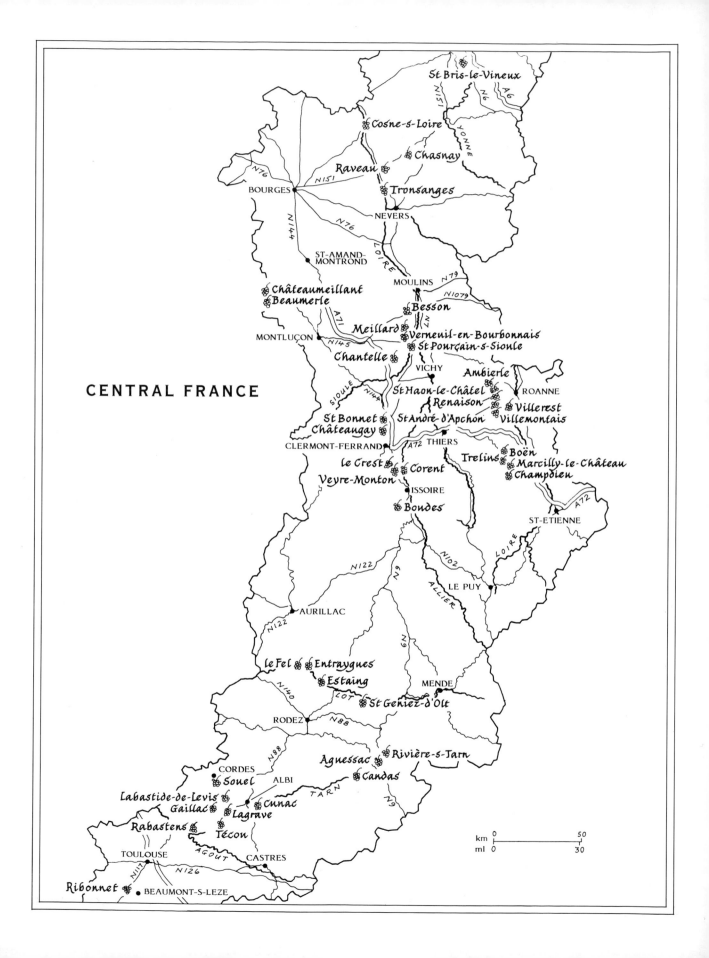

CENTRAL FRANCE

St Bris-le-Vineux

Cosne-s-Loire

Chasnay

Raveau

Tronsanges

BOURGES

NEVERS

ST-AMAND-MONTROND

MOULINS

Châteaumeillant
Beaumerle

Besson

Meillard

Verneuil-en-Bourbonnais
St Pourçain-s-Sioule

MONTLUÇON

Chantelle

VICHY

Ambierle

ROANNE

St Haon-le-Châtel
Renaison

Villerest
Villemontais

St Bonnet
Châteaugay

St André d'Apchon

CLERMONT-FERRAND

THIERS

Trelins

Boën
Marcilly-le-Château
Champbieu

le Crest

Corent

Veyre-Monton

ISSOIRE

ST-ETIENNE

Boudes

AURILLAC

LE PUY

le Fel

Entraygues

Estaing

MENDE

St Geniez-d'Olt

RODEZ

Aguessac

Rivière-s-Tarn

CORDES

Souel

ALBI

Candas

Labastide-de-Levis
Gaillac

Cunac

Lagrave

Rabastens

Técou

TOULOUSE

CASTRES

Ribonnet

BEAUMONT-S-LEZE

km 0   50
ml 0   30

This countryside, which borders the north-west of Burgundy, is one of sweeping rounded hills and broad vistas, and the vineyards occupy small plots within fields of wheat, maize and pasture land.

I visited Jean Jarreau in the pretty hamlet of Villemoison near St Père, where he farms about 8 hectares of vines producing red, white and rosé wines. He said ruefully that the effect of the VDQS appellation is to make him charge prices well below those of his more famous neighbours in Sancerre and Pouilly – even though his wines are very similar, both in terms of grape varieties and the terrain on which they are grown. There is talk that the Coteaux du Giennois may be elevated to AOC status in the not-far-distant future.

M. Jarreau makes red varietal wines from both Gamay and Pinot Noir, together with a rosé which is a blend of the two. In addition he makes a small quantity of Sauvignon Blanc from a total of one and a half hectares. It was being strictly rationed during my visit in 1992, because of the very bad frost the region suffered in the previous year which had reduced his harvest considerably.

The symbol used on many of the wine labels for the Coteaux du Giennois is derived from an emblem in the ancient Commanderie of the Knights Templars, which can be found on the outskirts of Villemoison.

Among the producers of Coteaux du Giennois there is an important INRA experimental station near Cours with a vineyard of about 10 hectares. Here wines produced on a commercial basis have received critical acclaim. At Les Loups near Bonny-sur-Loire, about 15 kilometres downstream, is the Domaine Joseph Balland-Chapuis, which has a sound reputation and is noted for its white and rosé wines. The Cave Coopérative at Pouilly-sur-Loire also produces a red and rosé Coteaux du Giennois from Pinot Noir in addition to AOC Pouilly-Fumé and Sancerre.

Other leading producers of Coteaux du Giennois include the Château de la Chaise at Thou, Jean Poupat & Fils at Gien, Alain Paulat at Villemoison, Jean-Paul Nerot and Jacques Carroue at Menetereau, Domaine des Ormousseaux at St Père and Veneau Frères at Cosne-Cours-sur-Loire.

SAUVIGNON DE ST BRIS

Although geographically separated, there is a small appellation in northern Burgundy, about 70 kilo-metres to the north-east, which bears more than a passing resemblance to the wines of the Loire. In a region where Chardonnay and Aligoté are used exclusively for white wine, the village of St Bris-le-Vineux has a VDQS appellation for a Sauvignon Blanc – Sauvignon de St Bris. The village is set in a particularly beautiful part of the Burgundian countryside a short distance to the south-west of Chablis. The neighbouring village of Irancy, set picturesquely in a hollow surrounded by steep hills, is famous for its AOC rosé wines.

COTEAUX CHARITOIS

One of the least known, and newest, Vins de Pays is to be found in the countryside to the east of La Charité-sur-Loire, about 14 kilometres upstream from Pouilly-sur-Loire in the *département* of Nièvre. The Vin de Pays des Coteaux Charitois was granted its appellation in 1986. At the time of writing there are only about 20 hectares of wines, but new plantings will double this within a few years.

The vineyards are situated around the villages of Raveau, Nanny, Chasnay, Murlin and La Celle-sur-Nièvre, around the edge of the Forêt des Bertranges, and also in the hamlet of Tronsanges on the right bank of the Loire a few kilometres south of La Charité.

Varietal red and white wines are made from Pinot Noir, Gamay, Sauvignon Blanc and Chardonnay. The largest vineyard is the Société des Hauts de Seyr at Chasnay, with 15 hectares, which was due to begin production of Chardonnay in 1993 and Pinot Noir in 1994.

I visited Daniel Pabion at his farm near the hamlet of Raveau, where he produces wines from about one and a half hectares of vines, which include Sauvignon Blanc, Gamay, Pinot Noir and Chardonnay. He makes a Vin Gris as well as a red from Pinot Noir, which is fermented in oak casks. His recently harvested Chardonnay, which had been fermenting for eight days at the time of my visit, already showed great promise.

M. René Renaud, at his farm near the hamlet of Tronsanges on the right bank of the Loire, has only a half hectare of vines as well as a large herd of Charolais and fields of maize. In addition to Gamay red, he produces white wine from Chasselas and Sauvignon

Overleaf: A meadow near Châteaumeillant in the *département* of Cher.

Blanc, sometimes a blend and sometimes individually, depending upon the harvest.

In the hamlet of Chasnay I tasted M. Roger Blouzat's Sauvignon Blanc, an excellent wine which, in addition to his Gamay, he produces entirely naturally and which can, he claims, be kept to advantage for a few years.

Nearby, on the main road, a large *caveaux* was being constructed for readiness in the spring of 1994 to market the wines of the Société des Hauts de Seyr. Few of the smaller producers have even roadside signs, however, and it is necessary to ask directions for the *vignerons* in the hamlets concerned.

Near Nevers, to the south of La Charité, the River Allier flows into the Loire from the south, and a short distance upstream on the left bank is the delightful village of Apremont-sur-Allier. It is hard to imagine a more tranquil setting: the village houses just a stone's throw from the wide grassy bank which borders the broad, slow-moving river; the water fringed by reeds and shaded by tall trees.

The houses are built of a warm, honey-coloured stone of which the region was an important source during the Middle Ages, with the river providing the mode of transportation. The stone was used for many important buildings, including the cathedral of Orléans. At one end of the village is an imposing fifteenth-century château, now housing a museum of horse-drawn carriages. It also has a magnificent floral park with gardens, lakes and cascades. One of the gardens is based on the famous white garden designed by Vita Sackville-West at Sissinghurst Castle in Kent.

About 50 kilometres south-west of Nevers is the Forêt de Tronçais, where much of the oak for wine casks originates. A short distance beyond is the upper valley of the Cher and its pretty tributary the Aumance. About 15 kilometres west of the Cher valley, on the D4 to Culan, is the rather nondescript village of Vesdun, which has gained fame by its claim to be the geographical centre of France. Although there has been some dispute in this matter, there is now a monument recording the claim, which has become something of a tourist attraction.

CHÂTEAUMEILLANT

The village of Vesdun is also one of the communities which owns the right to the small VDQS appellation of Châteaumeillant, a town some 20 kilometres to the west. In practice there is only 1 hectare of vines to be found in the vicinity of Vesdun, most of them being nearer to Châteaumeillant, around the villages of Feusines, Urciers, Champillet, Néret, St Maur, Reigny and Beaumerle.

There is a Cave Co-opérative on the outskirts of Châteaumeillant which has been in existence now for more than 30 years. It is responsible for the majority of production, although there are a few individual producers. Red wine from Gamay is made there, together with a Vin Gris from a blend of Gamay and Pinot Noir, while some white is produced and sold as Vin de Pays du Jardin de la France.

There are about 50 members of the co-operative, farming a total of about 50 hectares. The produce of the 15 hectares belonging to the Domaine des Garennes is vinified and bottled separately.

The classic wine of Châteaumeillant is considered to be the Vin Gris, a very pale rosé made by pressing the juice from black-skinned grapes before it has time to take on much colour.

Patrick Lanoix, of the Cellier du Chêne Combeau in the hamlet of Beaumerle, makes a particularly good Vin Gris from Gamay alone with a vineyard of about 6 hectares. He also makes a red 'Cuvée Spéciale' – using grapes from only his oldest Pinot Noir vines and keeping the wine in oak casks for a while before bottling – as well as a young-drinking red made from Gamay and a rosé from Pinot Noir. A Sauvignon Blanc is also made, which again is sold as Vin de Pays du Jardin de la France.

ST POURÇAIN-SUR-SIOULE

To the south-east of Châteaumeillant the River Allier flows north through Vichy from its source in the Cevennes. Like the Loire, of which it is a tributary, the Allier is also a wine river. On the western side of its broad valley between Vichy and Moulins, at the point where it is joined by the River Sioule, are the vineyards of the VDQS appellation, St Pourçain.

Vines have been grown here since before the Roman occupation, for it is recorded that the Phoenicians founded a colony at Chantelle and planted the first vines on the slopes overlooking the Bouble, a tributary of the Sioule. The Romans arrived in around 50BC, and at first continued to work the vineyards, but during the first century AD the Emperor Domitian banned the cultivation of vines and for more than two centuries wine-making ceased in the region.

During the Middle Ages the vines flourished again with the encouragement of the abbeys and were extended on to the slopes around the villages of Saulcet, Contigny and Montfand. At this time the wines of St Pourçain were considered worthy of comparison with those of Bordeaux, Burgundy and Champagne. They were transported throughout France by river and canal, and reached the tables of the highest in the land. Pope Clément VI, Charles VI and Henry VI are all recorded as being great admirers of the wines.

Towards the end of the eighteenth century the vineyards of St Pourçain covered more than 8,000 hectares, but today there are only about 800 hectares. Two-thirds of the total production is from the Cave Coopérative at St Pourçain, but there are over 20 individual producers. Most are members of the Caves Particulières association, whose distinctive brown and white signs at the road-side entice potential buyers.

The vineyards are planted on the low hills bordering the Allier, Bouble and Sioule rivers, and occupy a strip of land 5 kilometres wide and 30 kilometres long. The region was originally known for its white wines, and the region's distinctive grape variety was the Sacy, known locally as the Tresallier. It is a variety which was once widely planted in the Yonne and even began to rival Chardonnay in the Chablis region. It is still used as an element of some of the sparkling Crémant de Bourgogne made in that area.

Today, however, both Chardonnay and Sauvignon Blanc are used for white wines, although a proportion of Sacy is required under the appellation regulations and its inclusion is considered to be essential for a characteristic St Pourçain white wine. Both red and rosé wines made from Gamay and Pinot Noir have become increasingly important in the region and now account for three-quarters of the total production.

Bernard Gardien at Chassignoles, near the village of Besson, some 15 kilometres south-west of Moulins, has a vineyard of 18 hectares, of which 7 contain white grape varieties and 11 black. He produces a white wine with a blend of 80% Sauvignon Blanc and 20% Sacy and also makes a pure Chardonnay. Gamay is used for both red and rosé and another red wine is made from a blend of 80% Pinot Noir and 20% Gamay.

Georges Petillat, near the village of Meillard, a short distance to the south, has a vineyard of 15 hectares which was first planted by his father in 1922. He allows no Sacy in his white wine, using instead a blend of 75% Chardonnay and 25% Sauvignon Blanc. M. Petillat also makes red and rosé wines from Gamay and Pinot Noir.

Like M. Petillat, the Cave Co-opérative make a white from just Chardonnay and Sauvignon, but they produce a pure Sacy as well. A pure Pinot Noir is made here in addition to red and Vin Gris from Gamay, the latter also is used to make a Vin Nouveau which is released on 1 December. This is given the name La Ficelle, in memory of M. Gaultier, who owned a local tavern during the fifteenth century. He served his wines in large stoneware jugs, and in order to settle any arguments about how much had been consumed he used a piece of knotted string, *la ficelle*, to determine the exact amount.

St Pourçain is a pleasant riverside town where a lively country market takes places each Saturday in the church square. There is a museum of wine which is open from March until December; a wine festival is held each August, and a wine fair in February.

The countryside is a pleasure to explore, with its quiet lanes threading through a succession of slight hills and shallow valleys, its vineyards mingling with fields of grain and meadows dotted with creamy white Charolais cattle. Here and there, small châteaux can be seen in villages and hidden behind trees along the way.

A round trip of the southern part of the wine region can be made by following the D 415 road north-west from St Pourçain to the village of Saulcet, where there is a twelfth-century church. At Bransat, a little further west, there is an old stone bridge over the Gadenet. The route continues south-west to Chantelle, where one can see the remains of the fifteenth-century château of the Dukes of Bourbon, together with old timber-framed houses and a twelfth-century Romanesque church. A fine view of the village can be seen from the gorges of the little River Bouble nearby.

It is worth making a short detour south to the delightful walled village of Charroux, set on a hill overlooking the valley of the Sioule. During the Middle Ages it was one of the 19 manors of the Barony of Bourbon, and its ramparts and fortified gateways give a hint of its former importance. Today it is a sleepy and secretive place, with many old houses situated along its narrow cobbled streets, together with a

A village house in the St Pourçain wine village of Verneuil-en-Bourbonnais.

wash-house, ancient walls and castle ruins.

From Chantelle the wine route continues back to St Pourçain via the villages of Fourilles and Chareil, where there is an attractive château.

The northern section of the wine-growing region can be explored by following the road from Saulcet to Verneuil-en-Bourbonnais, a very pretty medieval village with a gateway and walls remaining from a feudal castle. There are many old timber-framed houses over five hundred years old, and a Romanesque church. On the outskirts of the village a very attractive old *pigeonnier* stands in a field.

From Verneuil the route continues northwards to Meillard, the château of Aix and a twelfth-century church, and on to Bresnay and Besson, where another twelfth-century church has been designated a national monument.

There are also three châteaux in the vicinity of the village: the fourteenth-century Vieux-Bost, hidden behind trees a short distance to the west; the fifteenth-century Château de Ristz, on the north-western edge of the village; and the very attractive Château de Four-chaud, south of the village on the D 292. The last has an impressive rectangular keep dating from the fourteenth century and is considered to be the finest example of a fortified house in the Bourbonnais.

CÔTES D'AUVERGNE

Some 60 kilometres higher up the valley of the River Allier from St Pourçain is the Côtes d'Auvergne, a wine-growing region of almost equal antiquity and one which was also of considerable importance during the Middle Ages.

The presence of vineyards in the Auvergne was mentioned by Sidonius Appollinaris, Bishop of Clermont, in the fifth century who likened them to those of Sicily. Records show that as early as the twelfth century the wines of Clermont were being transported by boat along the Allier and that they were being sold in the markets of Paris and consumed by the nobility during the centuries which followed.

In the seventeenth century the wines of the Auvergne were considered to be among the best in the land, with the *crus* of Chanturgue, Nérat, La Barre, Pompignac and Bourassol being singled out for special praise. At this time the dominant grape variety of the region was Burgundy's Pinot Noir, but in the eighteenth century these vines were replaced by Gamay, a variety which gave a greater yield and was better suited to the terrain.

In those days it was known as the wine of the *bougnats*, or coal merchants, as it was transported on roughly-built barges which were also loaded with coal, their departure timed to reach Paris before the end of the autumn flood. On arrival, both the wine and the coal were sold, together with the timber from the barge, which was broken up, and the bargee would then walk back to the Auvergne. This routine would be repeated each year until he had enough money to marry and settle down in Paris as a trader, selling the wares of his fellow *bougnats* still in the Auvergne.

The phylloxera blight reached the Auvergne considerably later than most other regions of France, providing an initial advantage, but when it did its effect was devastating. Before it arrived, in the late nineteenth century, the Auvergne vineyards had increased in the course of the century from about 18,000 to 60,000 hectares.

The destruction of phylloxera was followed by a plague-like attack of mildew in 1910. The vineyards' demise was accelerated during the next decade by the effects of the First World War and the gradual withdrawal of the labour force from agriculture as manufacturing industries like Michelin became established in Clermont-Ferrand. By the end of the 1920s the vineyards had shrunk to less than 15,00 hectares.

In 1936 the few remaining *vignerons* began to re-develop the vineyards on the most favoured slopes, and the renewal of the Vins d'Auvergne was under way. Now the plantations of vines are widely spaced between crops of maize, wheat and pasture land, and it is possible to drive south along the N 9 from Riom to St Germain-Lembron, through the heart of the wine-growing region, seeing only the occasional small plot of vines.

There are, surprisingly, more than 2,000 hectares in total, with the most important vineyards grouped in three main areas: around the town of Riom, to the south of Clermont-Ferrand, and in the countryside to the west of St Germain-Lembron. Just 500 hectares of these vines are delimited for the VDQS appellation of Côtes d'Auvergne which was granted in 1977, and elevation to AOC status is anticipated in the near future.

Gamay has remained the dominant grape variety, with about 95%, but plantings of Pinot Noir, Chardonnay and Sauvignon Blanc are regularly increasing. The wines are predominantly red, with about 40% made as rosé or Vin Gris.

There are still five defined *crus*: Madargues, around the town of St Bonnet-près-Riom; Châteaugay, near the village of that name about 10 kilometres to the south; Chanturgues, on the outskirts of Clermont-Ferrand; Corent, on the slopes around the hill village of that name; and around Boudes, a medieval village to the west of St Germain-Lembron.

The Cave Co-opérative at Veyre-Monton is responsible for about 45% of the total production, and the Côtes d'Auvergne organization lists 23 individual producers who account for most of the rest.

I visited M. Bernard Boulin-Constant, who has about 8 hectares of vines, three of which are Pinot Noir, on the slopes around the village of St Bonnet-près-Riom together with a newly-planted plot on the northern outskirts of Riom itself. He is one of just three producers in the area making the wine of Madargues, and was kind enough to take me out to his most favoured slopes a few kilometres from the village, where the distant Monts d'Auvergne create an impressive backdrop. There is a small plantation here of vines which were planted during the century's first decade, from which he makes a vine with the label 'Cuvée des Grandes Heures'.

The medieval hill village of Châteaugay lies about 10 kilometres south-west of Riom, overlooking the plain of Limagne. The wines made here had a considerable reputation during the Middle Ages and were, records attest, greatly appreciated by both Charles VI and Henry IV.

There are a number of *vignerons* making the *cru* of Châteaugay, of whom Pierre Lapouge and Michel and Raymond Rougeyron are the most important producers. The château, which dominates the small village, was built in the fourteenth century by Pierre de Giac, who was a member of the court of Charles VII. From the castle keep there is a splendid view of the plain of Limagne, the mountains of Forez and Livradois and the range of volcanic peaks which form the Chaîne des Puys.

Chanturgue is the smallest of the five *crus*, being produced from vines grown on the volcanic soil of the northern slopes of the 1,700-foot Puy de Chanturgue, now part of the suburbs of Clermont-Ferrand. Pierre Lapouge makes three-quarters of the average annual total of 200 hectolitres.

The village of Corent is set on a hill just east of Veyre-Monton. Terraces of vines occupy the steep slopes all around the village, which is an attractive cluster of old stone cottages and farms linked by a single narrow street. The *cru* of Corent is known especially for its rosé, and there are half a dozen or so producers in and around the village from whom the wines can be tasted and bought.

On the right bank of the Allier, a little to the north-east of Corent, is the Château de Busseol. Built by the comtes d'Auvergne in 1170, it is one of the oldest castles in the region.

I tasted an exceptionally good rosé in my hotel one evening and decided to track down the *vigneron*, Michel Blanc. The quest led me to another charming hilltop village, Le Crest, set on a hill a few kilometres north-west of Veyre-Monton with sweeping views of the surrounding countryside. In the ancient cellar below his village house I discovered that M. Blanc's red wine was just as good as his rosé.

A short distance south-west of Le Crest is another fascinating old village, St Saturnin, sheltering in the valley of the River Monne with a number of fine old houses and small manors. The village was the former residence of the barons of La Tour d'Auvergne, ancestors of the Medicis. On the edge of the village, there is an impressive fourteenth-century feudal castle with triple walls, machicolations, crenellated towers and ramparts. It is considered to be an outstanding example of medieval military architecture.

Nearby is the curious fortified village of La Sauvetat. Almost completely encircled by ramparts and threaded by a warren of narrow lanes, it is now partially derelict.

The countryside in this area is particularly appealing, with narrow country lanes winding through the rounded hills to small wine villages like Parent and Buron. Nearby is the delightful medieval village of

Montpeyroux, entered by a fortified gateway. At the eastern end of the village a thirteenth-century castle looks out over the valley of the Allier. For those seeking a quiet, comfortable hotel with excellent cuisine, only a stone's throw from the N 9, the atmospheric Auberge de Tralume is ideal.

The little village of St Floret lies only a dozen kilometres or so to the south-west of Montpeyroux in the peaceful valley of the Couze de Pavin. The village dates from the thirteenth century, when land here was given to an aide of the Dauphin. He took the name of St Floret and built a castle on the site. On a hill opposite the village is a fourteenth-century chapel which contains medieval wall paintings and a churchyard with ancient tombs carved into the rock.

About 20 kilometres east of St Floret, on the far side of the Allier valley, the ancient village of Usson is built on a rock which juts out abruptly from the plain. At the summit is a chapel with a monumental statue of the Virgin which was erected in the nineteenth century. Nearby are the remains of a feudal castle which, for 19 years, was the prison of Henry IV's wife, Marguerite de Valois, punished for an infidelity with a member of her husband's court.

The village of Boudes is set in the valley of the same name a short distance to the west of St Germain-Lembron. The old centre of the village, which dates from the eleventh century, has retained a strong medieval atmosphere, with its narrow streets and alleys, small square and an ancient church surrounded by old stone houses containing wine cellars.

One of these cellars contains the winery of André Charmensat, a leading producer of the *cru* of Boudes. He has about 8 hectares of vines, a quarter of which are young Pinot Noir, while some of his Gamay vines are more than 80 years old.

There are seven producers based in Boudes, farming a total of about 40 hectares of vines which are planted on the steep hillsides surrounding the village. Claude and Annie Sauvat have a vineyard of similar size to that of André Charmensat, mainly of Gamay but with a half hectare of Pinot Noir and a more recently planted hectare of Chardonnay.

Near Boudes, the Vallée des Saintes extends deep into the hills to the south of the village, providing a

Opposite: One of the medieval streets that encircle the church square of Bourdes in the Auvergne.

blissfully peaceful retreat for walkers and picnickers.

I visited the Domaine d'Hubel near the hamlet of St Herent, a short distance to the west of Boudes. Here, M. Hubel has less than two hectares of vines, with grain crops and cattle providing his main source of income. In spite of this, and the fact that his winery is a very simple, rustic affair, he was celebrating a gold medal just awarded by the Paris Concours Général for his red wine.

A few kilometres to the north of Boudes is the Château de Villeneuve, set on a ridge overlooking a peaceful valley. Built in the fourteenth century with a round tower in each corner, it contains a number of fifteenth-century frescoes, together with furniture and paintings of the period.

There is one small outpost of the Côtes d'Auvergne near the town of Billom, some 20 kilometres south-east of Clermont-Ferrand. Many of the small vineyards planted on the hillsides around the town are primarily for family consumption, but I found one commercial producer, Les Caves de l'Abbaye, in the attractive old village of Chauriat.

The community originally developed around a tenth-century priory. By the nineteenth century the village was surrounded by vineyards and had a thriving population of over 2,000. Many of the houses in the old quarter have wine cellars below. Les Caves de l'Abbaye are, appropriately enough, installed in an old church and, along with Côtes d'Auvergne, the speciality of Maison Dhôme has for several generations been the production of sparkling wine made by the *méthodé champenoise*.

A short distance to the south-east is the pretty hill village of Montmorin and, a little further to the east, the remains of the Château de Mauzun, a powerful fortress built on an outcrop of rock by the bishops of Clermont. From here there are sweeping views of the countryside, west to the Volcans and Les Monts Dore and east to the Monts du Forez.

CÔTES DU FOREZ

Further to the east of Billom is the Parc Livradois, a secretive countryside of densely wooded heights with shady valleys and meadows which are criss-crossed by numerous streams and rivers. The Monts du Forez

Opposite: A landscape in the Monts du Forez near the village of St Bonnet-de-Courreau in the *département* of Loire.

mark the division between this countryside and the wide valley of the Loire, and it is on the east-facing slopes of the hills which border the left bank of the river that the most southerly of the Loire vineyards can be found, the VDQS Côtes du Forez. They lie at altitudes ranging from 400 to 550 metres above sea level between the small town of Boën in the north and Montbrison, 17 kilometres to the south.

The production of Côtes du Forez is almost exclusively from the co-operative near the village of Trelins, just to the south of Boën. Before phylloxera there were more than 5,000 hectares of vines planted on the hillsides, but now there are just 200 hectares divided between 21 communes, which produce in the region of 8,000 hectolitres each year.

Only red and rosé wines are produced here, solely from Gamay, the variety of the Beaujolais region which lies only 60 kilometres or so to the north-east. The Côtes du Forez was granted VDQS status in 1956 and the co-operative was established six years later. It now has over 200 hundred members, of whom only a few make a living exclusively from their vines. It is a very fertile region and the valley floor, if not pasture land, is planted with orchards and cereal crops.

Five grades of wines are produced: a red *primeur*, which is on sale from December; 'Cuvée Traditionelle', which is made as red, rosé *sec* and rosé *demi-sec*; a special *cuvée* made with the grapes from vines grown on volcanic soil and named after a different selected writer each year; 'Cuvée Prestige', which is made with grapes from the oldest vines; and 'Cuvée Pierre Dellenbach', which is produced from one particular vineyard on especially favoured terrain and vinified separately.

The co-operative also makes a red Vin de Pays d'Urfé, from Gamay vines grown outside the delimited areas for the Côtes du Forez; and a small quantity of white Vin de Pays is also produced from relatively recent plantings of Chardonnay.

The principal wine villages are Trelins – near which is the sixteenth-century château of Goutelas – Marcoux, Marcilly – where there is a thirteenth-century château perched on a hill above the vineyards – Pralong and Champdieu, a pretty walled village with ramparts, gateways and a fourteenth-century fortified church.

A tour of some of the most scenic parts of the Monts du Forez can be made by following the D 496 south-west from Montbrison to St Anthème, where the D 139

leads north to the Col des Supeyres. From here the road winds its way down to Ambert, which is famous for its blue cheese, Fourme d'Ambert. *En route* you will pass the ancient paper mill of Moulin Richard de Bas, where you can still see paper being made.

From Ambert you can follow the River Dore downstream to Vertolaye, and head eastwards on the D 268 and then the D 40, which winds through splendid scenery over the Col du Béal to the old village of Chalmazel to see the impressive thirteenth-century Château de Talru-Marcilly.

From here, the route descends into the valley of the Couzan, where the remains of another ruined château can be seen on a pinnacle of rock 610 metres above, before returning to Boën. A few kilometres to the south-east of Boën is the Bastie d'Urfé, a medieval castle which was rebuilt in the sixteenth century in the Italian Renaissance style.

Another scenic route starts at Verrières-en-Forez, which lies about half-way between Montbrison and St Anthème. The quiet D 44 leads north through a succession of attractive valleys and hillsides towards St Bonnet-de-Courreau, from where you can enjoy stunning views over the Forez landscape, before descending either to Marcoux or Pralong.

CÔTES ROANNAISES

From Boën it is only a short drive north to the vineyards of the Côtes Roannaises which, like the Côtes du Forez, lie on the slopes to the west of the Loire valley. A very enjoyable route between the two regions can be made by following the D 8 north of Boën to Bussy-Albieux, where the D 42 leads north-east to Pommiers, an attractive fortified village which has a priory and a church with frescoes dating from the fifteenth century.

Beyond, at St Paul-de-Vézelin, the D 26 crosses the Loire at the southern end of the gorges, which were dammed to create a reservoir, and a very attractive route continues north along the right bank of the lake towards Roanne. The Château de la Roche once stood on a rocky outcrop above the Loire gorges, but it is now marooned on the lake with only a narrow causeway linking it to the mainland. Like Venice, it is threatened by subsidence, and efforts are currently being made to prevent it disappearing into the lake.

A few kilometres south of Roanne you can cross the river, where it is dammed, to Villerest, a very pretty

Above: A house in the Côtes Roannaises wine village of St Haon-le-Châtel. Overleaf: The village of Conques in the *département* of Aveyron.

medieval village with a network of ancient narrow streets which is set on a hill overlooking the lake.

The vineyards of the Côtes Roannaises extend along the foothills of the Monts de la Madeleine from the left bank of the Loire at Villerest and St Maurice to Changy, about 20 kilometres to the north-west. Like many French vineyards, they were first established by the monasteries during the Middle Ages, and between the thirteenth and sixteenth centuries they continued to expand vigorously, with the Loire providing a ready means of transport to Paris.

Today there are around 130 hectares of vines distributed between 24 communes, but unlike the Côtes du Forez all of the wines are produced by individual growers and there is no Cave Co-opérative. Red and rosé wines are produced exclusively from a variety of Gamay, which is known locally as St Romain à Jus Blanc. The principal wine villages are St Maurice-sur-Loire, Villerest, Villemontais, St André-d'Apchon, Renaison, St Haon-le-Châtel, St Haon-le-Vieux and Ambierle.

URFÉ

I visited Robert Chaucesse, whose vineyards high on the slopes above the village of Renaison have been in his family since the beginning of the seventeenth century – it is one of the oldest *domaines* of the region. In addition to his award-winning red and rosé Côtes Roannaises, M. Chaucesse also makes a Vin de Pays d'Urfé from a small plot of Chardonnay.

Other notable producers of Côtes Roannaises include Jean-Baptiste Clair at Le Chambon, Antoine Néron at the Coteaux de la Rochette near Ville-montais, the Domaine de la Paroisse near Pomport, the Domaine des Millets at Lentigny, Michel Mont-roussier and Felix Vial in the village of St André-

d'Apchon, Robert Sérol near Renaison, and the Domaine du Pavillon at Ambierle.

The village of St Haon-le-Châtel still retains part of its ramparts as well as a fortified gateway and a number of fine old houses. There is a *caveau* here where the Côtes Roannaises wines can be tasted and bought. At Ambierle, a short distance to the north, there is a fine Gothic church, with a beautiful multicoloured roof of mosaic tiles, and a museum of folk art and local traditions.

The tiny walled village of Le Crozet, a little further to the north, was the property of the vicomtes de Macon in the tenth century and became the domain of the comtes de Forez in the thirteenth century, when it was fortified. Entered by a gateway flanked by towers, it has narrow winding streets and numerous sixteenth-century houses, one of which has been made into a museum of local history. The town hall is situated in the fifteenth-century Maison du Connétable, a beautiful timber-fronted building with arcades which was formerly the shoe-makers' hall.

The best of the Monts de la Madeleine countryside can be explored by following the quiet country roads which link the villages of Le Crozet, Arfeuilles, Châtel-Montagne, Le Mayet-de-Montagne, St Nicolas-des-Biefs, St André-d'Apchon, Renaison and St Haon-le-Châtel. The road from St André-d'Apchon towards Arcon has some especially fine views over the Roannais countryside and valley of the Loire. Beyond Arcon is the curious outcrop of rock known as the Rocher de Rochefort, from where there are stunning views over the Rouchain valley.

To the south-west of the Côtes Roannaises is the Pays d'Urfé, from which the local Vin de Pays takes its name. A few kilometres to the south-east of St Just-en-Cheval are the remains of the Château d'Urfé. It takes about half an hour to walk up to the site, but on a clear day it is worth it, because you can see the distant Alps to the east. A short distance to the west, set on a hill, is the charming walled village of Cervières, which retains some ramparts as well as a fifteenth-century church and fine old Renaissance houses.

ENTRAYGUES ET DU FEL

From its source in the Cevennes near Bagnols-les-Bains, not far from that of the Tarn, the River Lot runs an almost parallel course for much of its length before, like the Tarn, flowing into the Garonne.

The Lot is a wine river of some renown. The 'black wine' of Cahors was at one time a serious competitor to those from Bordeaux, and it is claimed that the popes insisted that the wine of Cahors be used for the celebration of Mass. Not all of the Lot wines come from the reach between Cahors and Fumel, however, and there are two small VDQS appellations for wines produced in the upper Lot valley, one at each end of the Lot gorges.

The attractive little market town of Entraygues is set at the confluence of the Lot and the Truyère. A medieval stone bridge crosses the Truyère, and there is a castle on the bank of the Lot where tree-shaded meadows reach down to the water's edge. The town is surrounded by steep rounded hills which in late summer are tinted bright purple with heather but once were covered with vines. The wine-making tradition of the region was greatly encouraged in the Middle Ages by the monks of the abbey of Conques, and remains of the stone terraces used to retain the soil on the steep slopes are still visible.

Before phylloxera there were over a thousand hectares of vines on the hillsides, but now there are just a handful of producers and only about 20 hectares of vines. I visited M. Walthus, whose 6 hectares of vines are grown on the steep hillside to the north of the town above the left bank of the Truyère.

He told me that the appellation is best known for its white wine, and that his own is made from a blend of Chenin Blanc and a local variety, Plantagenet. He also makes a red wine from 60% Cabernet Sauvignon, 30% Fer Servadou and 10% Negret – for the colour, he says – and a rosé from 100% Gamay. François Avallon, in the neighbouring hamlet of St Georges, is also known for his white wine, which is made from pure Chenin Blanc.

The full name of the appellation is Vin d'Entraygues et du Fel, the latter referring to the hamlet of Le Fel, a cluster of old stone houses and farms which is set at the summit of a lofty sheer-sided hill overlooking the River Lot. It's a delightfully peaceful spot, and there is a small *auberge* located in the middle of the village which provides a truly rural retreat with good simple food and accommodation. It belongs to the Logis network and is part of a chain of similar small hotels linking walks through the Chataignerie, the

Opposite: The wine village of Estaing on the banks of the River Lot.

high-ridge chestnut country of the region.

An essential excursion to make in this region is to the village of Conques, about 20 kilometres to the south-west. The route follows the winding wooded valley of the Lot with constantly pleasing views of the muddy brown river to the old village of Vieillevie. A few kilometres beyond, the River Dourdou emerges from a steep wooded valley to join the Lot. A little way up the valley of the Dourdon, high on a hillside, is Conques, a collection of honey-coloured houses tiered in zig-zag pattern up the steep slope. There is scarcely a level inch of ground in the village, and the houses are built on terraces carved into the hillside and linked by winding lanes and steps.

At the foot of the village, set on a natural platform, is the lovely old abbey church of Sainte Foy, with its towers soaring above the steeply-pitched brown tiled roofs. The surprising scale of the building, which seems to dwarf the village, is explained by the fact that the relics of a young martyr, Sainte Foy, were brought to the abbey at Conques after being stolen from their original home in the abbey of Agen. As a result the church of Sainte Foy became an important place of pilgrimage during the Middle Ages and was a staging-post on the route to Santiago de Compostela, bringing considerable wealth and prosperity to the community. The church still houses one of the most valuable collections of medieval religious treasures in the world.

There is a splendid view of Conques from the Site de Bancarel, which can be reached from a small road leading off the D 901 to Marcillac. This is delightful countryside, with steep rounded hills cut by narrow valleys and numerous rivers and streams sheltered by wooded banks.

There are a number of delightfully unspoiled villages in the area south of Entraygues, notably Salles-la-Source, with its impressive cascade, Muret-le-Château, the curious village of Bozouls, built on the edge of a huge pot-hole in the River Dourdou, and the little *bastide* of Villecomtal.

The market town of Marcillac is known for its AOC wines, and there is Cave Co-opérative on the N 140 near Valady, as well as a number of independent producers in the surrounding villages.

ESTAING

From Villecomtal the D 22 climbs up over the hills before descending steeply into the valley of the Lot to enter the village of Estaing. This is one of the prettiest riverside villages in France, with a château set above the rooftops of the village houses and a fine old stone bridge spanning the Lot.

The castle belonged to François d'Estaing, Bishop of Rodez, who financed the construction of one of the great towers of its cathedral from his revenues, and whose statue can be seen on the bridge. A fête is held on the first Sunday in July when the villagers, dressed in medieval costume, process through the narrow streets to the church.

Like Entraygues, the vineyards surrounding Estaing have their own VDQS appellation, which was granted in 1965. A group of six producers have formed a small co-operative, the Caveau du Viala, farming about 12 hectares of vines, which makes it the smallest co-operative and VDQS appellation in France. The co-operative's winery can be found in a small industrial estate a short distance to the north of the village below the steep terraced hillsides on which the vines are planted.

A basic red wine is made here from 60% Gamay with a balance of Pinot Noir and Negrette, while a 'Cuvée Prestige' is produced from 80% Cabernet Sauvignon and 20% Fer Servadou. A blend of 70% Gamay and 30% Jurançon Noir is used to make a rosé, and the white wine is produced from 70% Chenin Blanc and 30% Mauzac.

Up river from Estaing the D 920 leads to the riverside town of Espalion, after which the valley route continues along the D 6 to the old walled village of St Côme-d'Olt and then over the hills before descending again to the river valley near St Geniez-d'Olt. Best known for its strawberries, the small agricultural co-operative in the village also sells the wines of Estaing.

A few kilometres downstream from St Geniez is the enchanting little village of Ste Eulalie-d'Olt. Dating from the twelfth century, the village has a wealth of old houses, a pretty church, modelled on Ste Foy at Conques, and two small châteaux. A festival and procession are held here on the second Sunday in July to celebrate the two thorns preserved in the church, which are said to be from Christ's crown and were brought here by the feudal lord on his return from the seventh crusade.

Opposite: The Tarn gorges near Millau in the *département* of Aveyron.

Harvesting the grapes in the gorges of the Tarn.

GORGES ET CÔTES DE MILLAU

The River Tarn is one of the most beautiful in France. Rising in in the Lozère mountains, it passes through enormously varied countryside on its way to join the Garonne beyond Moissac. From its source as far as Florac, it is a mountain river fed by streams and underground springs, but as it descends it enters a great rift between the limestone plateaux of the Causses de Méjean and the Causse de Sauveterre, creating one of the great sights of France, the Tarn Gorges.

Downstream of the gorges is the busy town of Millau, where the main industry is based on goat and sheepskins. Although, at first sight, there is little sense of being in wine-growing country, the region has its own appellation of Vins de Pays. Formerly known as Aveyron, it is now called Gorges et Côtes de Millau.

The Cave Co-opérative, based in the small town of Aguessac a few kilometres to the north of Millau, is the driving force behind the commercialization of the local wines and has a *caveau* where they can be tasted

before buying, both *en vrac* and in bottles.

Wine-making has a long tradition in this region. The ruins of the château in the neighbouring village of Compeyre once guarded a wealthy cave-dwelling community which, during the Middle Ages, was responsible for the making, storing and selling of all the region's wines, and in those times the valley was filled with vines.

The Gamay de Beaujolais was the favoured variety during the Middle Ages and it still represents a large proportion of the planting. Here it is known as the Gamet du Pape. During the period of the popes of Avignon the nearby village of Mostuéjouls had an impressive château, and one of its lords was made a cardinal in the pope's court. Each year when returning to Avignon he would take with him a supply of the local wine. It is said that the pope would have no other wine on his table and, as a result, for more than 600 years the vines have been known as Gamet du Pape.

During the Wars of Religion the village was

destroyed, and it never regained it prosperity, but the caves remain and are still used today for storing wine. In 1850, before phylloxera, the vineyards covered 15,000 hectares, and there is evidence of an active export trade from Compeyre and Rivière-sur-Tarn to New York which continued until 1870. The onslaught of phylloxera followed by the First World War and the loss of more than 500 *vignerons* from the valley, signalled the end of the region's wine industry.

Replanting of the vines began in 1960, and in 1966 the appellation was created. The co-operative, claimed to be the smallest in France – although this, as we have seen, is hotly contested – was established in 1980, and today the Gamet du Pape is supplemented by Syrah and Cabernet Sauvignon together with local black and white grape varieties.

The co-operative makes a red wine from a blend of 40% Gamay, 30% Syrah and 20% Cabernet Sauvignon, with the balance made up of the traditional varieties, Tanat, Cot, Duras and Negrette. A 'Cuvée des Affineurs' is also produced with 60% Cabernet Sauvignon, 20% traditional varieties and the balance of Syrah and Gamay.

A rosé is made using 50/50 Gamay and Cabernet Sauvignon and a white from 70% Chenin Blanc and 30% Mauzac. Considerable care is taken over quality control, and the yield is restricted to 60 hectolitres per hectare, less than many Vins de Pays. There are just three independent producers, based in Rivière-sur-Tarn, to the north of Millau, and at Candas and St Georges-de-Luzençon, both to the west of it.

The vineyards extend along the narrow valley in small pockets for 80 kilometres between Peyreleau and Conac, to the west near Réquista, through some of the most spectacular scenery in France. From Compeyre to Peyreleau the vineyards can be seen along both sides of the valley, and the D 907 on the right bank provides splendid views. The small quiet road which leads from Millau along the left bank through vineyards and orchards to the pretty village of La Cresse on its way to Peyreleau offers a delightful alternative.

From Peyreleau you can make a truly breath-taking round trip through the Tarn Gorges to the villages of Les Vignes, La Malène and Ste Enimie before crossing the Tarn and traversing the Causse Méjean to the picturesque little riverside town of Meyrueis. From here the D 996 returns to Peyreleau through the beautiful Jonte Gorges.

A *vigneron* in the vineyards of the Tarn gorges.

Downstream from Millau the D 41 follows the river along the right bank, offering a succession of beautiful views on its way to the little wine village of Candas. A detour from here along the D 96 to St Beauzély provides more stirring sights, including the dramatically sited village of Castelnau-Pégayrols, perched on a steep rocky escarpment.

From St Beauzély the D 30 and D 993 lead back to the river at St Rome-de-Tarn. The route continues to follow the river via the villages of Le Truel and Broquiès to Brousse-le-Château, a tiny village with a château and church surrounded by ancient houses, set on a steep domed rock at the confluence of the Tarn and the Alrance. Le Relais de Chasteau offers simple accommodation and good food at a modest price beside the river.

Beyond the old town of Ambialet, held in a wide meander of the river, the Tarn flows onwards to Albi, which lies at the edge of the plain of Toulouse. The old centre of the city is delightful, with its massive red-brick cathedral soaring above the houses and the ancient bridge – claimed to be the oldest in France – which spans the Tarn.

The Palace de la Berbie adjacent to the cathedral contains a collection of Toulouse-Lautrec's work which the artist donated to his home town. Don't miss seeing the delightful small garden in the cathedral enclosure, with its rose arbours, ornamental borders, statues and plane trees, or the magnificent view of the Tarn and its bridge from the battlements.

CÔTES DU TARN

To the west of Albi is the little town of Gaillac, renowned for its AOC wines, which were recognized in 1938, and also for its very well-known Vin de Pays, Côtes du Tarn. It is one of the oldest vineyards in France, originally planted during the first century AD. In the tenth century it was taken under the wing of the monks of the Abbey of St Michel de Gaillac and from the twelfth to the fourteenth century its wine was exported to England, Holland and Belgium.

The vineyards extend on both banks of the Tarn, to the north as far as Cordes, south to Giroussens, west to Rabastens, and east to Bellegarde, the other side of Albi. The soil of the left bank is gravelly and is used largely to produce red wines, while the hillier country to the north harbours the more favoured vineyards.

The dominant variety for the white wines is Mauzac, together with another local variety seldom found elsewhere, the Len de l'El. Muscadelle, Sauvignon Blanc, Semillon and Ondenc are also grown. Plantings of the black-skinned varieties include Duras, Braucal, Merlot, the Cabernets, Syrah and, growing increasingly in popularity, Gamay.

Like the Côtes de Gascogne, the Côtes du Tarn has become a major export success and done much to help create an identity for the more modestly-priced wines of France. Again like the Côtes de Gascogne, it largely owes its marketing success to one particular Cave Co-opérative, at the village of Labastide-de-Lévis, between Gaillac and Albi.

It was created in 1949 by a group of 80 *vignerons* with the aim of restoring the ancient vineyards of Gaillac. Today it has 412 members, representing 10% of the total area of vineyards, and is established as the

Opposite: Vineyards of the Côtes du Tarn near the hill village of Cordes.

largest producer of AOC Gaillac wines. In 1957 it created the co-operative at Cunac, a few kilometres east of Albi, and in 1974 incorporated the Cave du Pays Cordais near the village of Souel.

At the Labastide-de-Lévis co-operative, white Côtes du Gascogne is produced from a blend of Mauzac, Len de l'El and Muscadelle. A rosé is made from 100% Jurançon, and a red from 65% Jurançon and 35% Portugais Bleu. At Cunac a Gamay red is produced using carbonic maceration, as well as a *primeur* using the same variety. A Blanc Moelleux is also made from the Semillon variety. Most of the Vin de Pays wines are available in conventional 75cl bottles, screw-capped 1 litre bottles and *en vrac*.

I also visited the co-operative at Rabastens, where basic red, white and rosé Côtes de Gascognes are sold *en vrac*, and superior red and rosé in bottles. These are made from a blend of Duras, Merlot, Cabernet Franc, Cabernet Sauvignon, Brancol and Syrah, with the label Henri de Cambourne.

At the Cave de Técou, a few kilometres south-east of Gaillac, red and rosé of 100% Jurançon are produced, as well as a white from Mauzac and Muscadelle with a little Len de l'El.

Alain Bounes at the Domaine de Guiroudets, near the village of Lagrave, is an independent producer who sells a small quantity of Vins de Pays in bottles and *en vrac*, in addition to his AOC Gaillac. From a total of 22 hectares he makes Gamay red, a rosé from 100% Syrah and a white from a blend of Muscadelle, Len de l'El and Ugni Blanc, with just a little Sauvignon Blanc.

A tour of the vineyards will also lead you to some of the most attractive countryside and picturesque villages in this part of France. From Gaillac the D 964 leads north-west to the little hill-top village of Castelnau-de-Montmirail. A *bastide* built in the thirteenth century, it has a very pretty restored square, surrounded by arcades, at the centre of a web of narrow streets with timber-framed houses. The Gothic church contains a Byzantine cross studded with precious stones.

The road continues westwards into the valley of the Vère to another spectacularly sited hilltop village, Puycelci. Less restored than Castelnau, its old streets contain numerous houses from the fourteenth and fifteenth centuries as well as a good Gothic church. There are stunning views from the battlements across the valley to the Forêt de Grésigne.

A few kilometres north-west of Puycelci is the fortified village of Bruniquel, set on a cliff above the River Aveyron. At the summit is a castle which was built more than 700 years ago. The original castle was named after Brunehaut, a Carolingian princess, which is how the village got its present name.

A few kilometres up river there is another dramatic sight, the fortress of Penne, surmounting a jagged crest of rock, while the village with its narrow streets, old houses and fortified gateways is laid out below.

A little further upstream on the right bank of the Aveyron is St Antonin-Noble-Val, a small spa town set very prettily beside the river, which is spanned by an attractive old bridge. Inside, the atmosphere is distinctly medieval, with dark narrow streets and numerous ancient houses, some dating from the thirteenth century, together with a Romanesque town hall which was restored by Viollet-le-Duc.

From St Antonin the D 19 and D 91 lead south-east to Cordes, the city in the sky. Built on a steep rounded hill above the valley of the Cerou, it is the quintessential medieval stronghold with steep cobbled streets, fortified gateways, battlements, towers and a wealth of fine old buildings. The village also possesses an outstanding hôtel-restaurant, Le Grand Ecuyer, where master chef Yves Thuries offers his culinary skills daily and you can sleep in a four-poster bed.

A quiet scenic route back through the vineyards to Labastide-de-Lévis can be enjoyed by following the D 30, just to the south of Cordes, to Noailles, Cestayrols and Fayssac.

HAUTE-GARONNE

Beyond the southern limit of the Gaillac vineyards there is little vine culture until the Côtes de la Malapère are reached to the west of the city of Carcassonne.

In the *département* of Haute-Garonne, however, there are a few small outposts to the south of the city of Toulouse. The Domaine de Ribonnet is situated in a region of big rounded hills to the west of the valley of the Lèze near the village of Beaumont-sur-Lèze.

Here, in the midst of a 220-hectare estate which surrounds a fifteenth-century château, 33 hectares of vines are under cultivation. The château was the home of Clémant Adler, an ingenious engineer and inventor of the last century who successfully completed a 50-metre flight in his single-engined aircraft named Eole 1. He lived at the Domaine de Ribonnet until 1923,

The Château de Ribbonet near Beaumont-sur-Lèze in the *département* of Haute-Garonne.

giving much of his attention to its vineyards and cellar.

The property is now owned by Christian Gerber and his family. They are not allowed to use the title of Château de Ribbonet on the labels, however, since Haute-Garonne is only a Vins de Pays appellation and the wines are labelled Domaine de Ribonnet. A vast range of noble grape varieties vines are grown here – Cabernet Sauvignon, Cabernet Franc, Merlot, Pinot Noir, Gamay, Sauvignon Blanc, Semillon, Chasselas, Sylvaner, Riesling, Gewürztraminer, Pinot Gris, Chardonnay, Aligoté and Marsanne!

The current (1993) tariff lists varietal red wines from Cabernet Sauvignon, Pinot Noir and Merlot together with 'Cuvée Clémant Adler', which is blended from Cabernet Sauvignon, Merlot and Cabernet Franc and allowed to mature in oak casks for up to 15 months before bottling. Varietal rosés are made from Syrah, Merlot and Cabernet Franc, and white *vins de cépage* are produced from Chardonnay and Marsanne – both oak-aged – as well as a Riesling and a Gewürztraminer.

SOUTH-EAST FRANCE

Opposite: Vineyards near the Dentelles de Montmirail.
Above: The hill village of Roussillon.

Like most French *départements*, the Ardèche is named after the river which runs through it. It is one of the loveliest of all France's waterways, a sinuous fast-flowing river which, in turn, runs over white-stone beds, through steep, narrow gorges and between high, densely-wooded banks.

CÔTES DU VIVARAIS

The Ardèche rises in the northern Cevennes below the summit of Mont Mazenc in the Forêt de Mazan. The rivers Lot and Tarn also rise not far away, but while they lead west towards the Atlantic the Ardèche rises on the other side of the watershed and flows south-east to join the Rhône near Pont-St-Esprit.

North of Pont-St-Esprit on the west bank of the Rhône is the town of Viviers, with an attractive and well-preserved old quarter of cobbled streets and ancient buildings. The town gives its name to the mountainous region crossed by the Ardèche on its way from the Cevennes to the Rhône valley, known as the Vivarais.

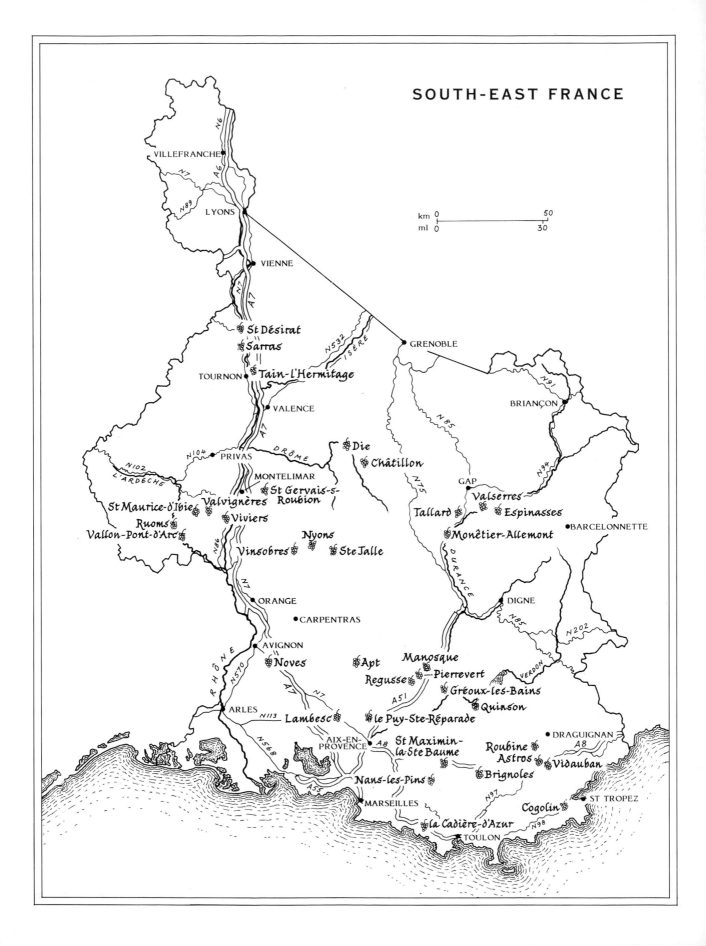

SOUTH-EAST FRANCE

km 0   50
ml 0   30

VILLEFRANCHE

LYONS

VIENNE

GRENOBLE

St Désirat
Sarras
Tain-l'Hermitage
TOURNON

VALENCE

BRIANÇON

DRÔME
Die
Châtillon

PRIVAS
L'ARDÈCHE

MONTELIMAR
St Gervais-s-
Roubion
Valvignères
Viviers

GAP
Valserres
Tallard
Espinasses

BARCELONNETTE

St Maurice-d'Ibie
Ruoms
Vallon-Pont-d'Arc

Nyons
Vinsobres
Ste Jalle

Monêtier-Allemont

DURANCE

ORANGE

CARPENTRAS

DIGNE

RHÔNE

AVIGNON
Noves

Apt
Regusse
Manosque
Pierrevert
Gréoux-les-Bains
Quinson

VERDON

ARLES
Lambesc
le Puy-Ste-Réparade

AIX-EN-
PROVENCE
St Maximin-
la-Ste Baume

DRAGUIGNAN

Roubine
Astros
Vidauban
Brignoles

Nans-les-Pins

MARSEILLES

Cogolin
ST TROPEZ

la Cadière-d'Azur

TOULON

The countryside, which ranges from luxuriant valleys to stony *garrigues* and wooded mountains, is also densely cultivated with vines. The Côtes du Vivarais has been a VDQS appellation since 1962 and covers the terrain around the following 14 villages: Barjac, Bidon, Gras, Issirac, Labastide-de-Virac, Lagorce, Larnas, Le Garn, Montclus, St Privat-de-Champclos, Vinezac, Organac-l'Aven, St Montant and St Remèze – of which the final three are also entitled to the appellation of *cru.*

The principal permitted grape varieties are Grenache Noir, Syrah, Cinsaut, Auban and Carignan for red and rosé wines; Marsanne, Clairette, Bourboulenc, Macabeau, Mauzan, Picpoul, Ugni Blanc and Grenache Blanc for white wines.

There are numerous independent producers, of whom nearly 70 belong to the organization of Caves Particuliers which provides each member vineyard with distinctive brown and white signs depicting a *vigneron* carrying a barrel on his shoulders. Nearly 40 Cave Co-opératives are also distributed throughout the region.

The Vignerons Ardèchois, based at Ruoms, some 25 kilometres south of Aubenas, incorporates 20 of the co-operatives and has a very progressive approach to commercialization and marketing. It represents over 3,000 *vignerons* farming nearly 6,000 hectares of vines, and has a total *cuverie* capacity of 700,000 hectolitres, of which 36,000 are at the Ruoms co-operative. Here the red and rosé Côtes du Vivarais wines are made from a blend of 50% Grenache Noir, 30% Syrah and 10% each of Cinsaut and Carignan, using 80% traditional fermentation and 20% carbonic maceration. The white Côtes de Vivarais is produced from about 30 hectares of vines planted on the stony terraces of the lower Vivarais using a blend of Grenache Blanc, Clairette and Ugni Blanc.

COTEAUX DE L'ARDÈCHE

In addition to VDQS wines the region also has a Vin de Pays appellation, Coteaux de l'Ardèche. Although a proportion of these wines are made using a blend of grape varieties, many producers take the opportunity to make *vins de cépage* and to use varieties not permitted under VDQS regulations.

At Ruoms, for example, a red is made using a blend of Grenache, Syrah, Cabernet Sauvignon, Cinsaut and Merlot as well as *vins de cépage* from Syrah, Merlot,

Cabernet Sauvignon and Chardonnay. The co-operative also produces a Vin de Pays du Comté de Grignan, from Grenache, Syrah and Cabernet Sauvignon together with a small proportion of Cinsaut, as well as a similarly constructed Vin de Pays des Comtés Rhodaniens, which is produced using biological methods.

Near the village of Vallon-Pont-d'Arc, just above the Ardèche Gorges, is the Domaine du Colombier, where Philippe and Alain Walbaum farm 27 hectares of vines along the banks of the River Ardèche. The terrain falls just outside the area defined for the VDQS appellation, so only Vin de Pays is made here. The Walbaums make what they call a 'Rouge Tradition' from a blend of Syrah, Grenache Noir and Carignan, a 'Cuvée Spéciale' from just Grenache and Syrah, together with a rosé from pure Syrah.

Unlike many of the local *vignerons* who make Vin de Pays, Alain Walbaum favours the traditional local varieties in preference to non-indigenous vines like Cabernet or Chardonnay. He has, however, recently planted 2 hectares of Merlot and 3 of Viognier, a variety which is becoming quite popular with growers in the Ardèche. The vineyard was planted by his grandfather in 1860 and in the cottages and outbuildings near the fine old farmhouse are seven well-appointed *gîtes.*

From the village of Vallon-Pont-d'Arc a road leads northwards along the valley of the River Ibie to the picturesque villages of Les Salelles and St Maurice-d'Ibie. It's a quiet, secluded valley, with the small river winding between outcrops of rock over a bed of white stones. In the middle of the valley is the Mas de la Bégude, a very attractive old farmhouse where Gilles Azzoni and his wife produce both Côtes de Vivarais and Vins de Pays de l'Ardèche from 8 hectares of vines planted on the valley floor and the slopes either side.

Côtes du Vivarais is made here from a blend of 70% Syrah and 30% Grenache, but the Vin de Pays includes a pure Merlot, a rosé from 60% Cinsaut and 40% Grenache, a white from 90% Roussanne and 10% Viognier, as well as a pure Viognier which is allowed to mature for six months in oak casks. M. Azzoni told me that he was the first to introduce Viognier into this part of the Ardèche and has enjoyed considerable success with it.

Overleaf: The valley of Valvignères and the vineyards of the Coteaux de l'Ardèche.

Between Les Salelles and St Maurice-d'Ibie a small road leads eastwards over the steep *garrigue*-covered hills before descending, with sweeping views, into the valley of Valvignères. This is a much larger and wider valley than the Ibie and is carpeted with vines as far as the eye can see. Its name is derived from the Latin, Vallis Vinaria – valley of the vines – for wine-making was already in progress here 2,000 years ago, when the region was the centre of the Gallo-Roman province of Helvie.

The wines were transported as far as Lyons, Rome and even to the Low Countries, where an amphora was discovered bearing the name Helvorium. The little walled village of Valvignères is one of the loveliest in the region with a pretty church, a clock tower and small squares with many old stone houses linked by narrow streets and passages.

The valley has its own Cave Co-opérative, which was formed in 1951 and today is supported by nearly 120 *vignerons* making both Côtes du Vivarais and Vin de Pays. In addition to the traditional grape varieties used for the VDQS wines, recent plantings include both Chardonnay and Viognier for *vins de cépage*.

A few kilometres to the south of Valvignères is the Mas d'Intras, where Alphonse Robert and his son produce Vin de Pays des Coteaux de l'Ardèche from 16 hectares of vines which they established at the start of the 1980s after having left the co-operative.

A blended red is made from Grenache, Syrah, Merlot and Cabernet Sauvignon, as well as a Merlot/Syrah which won a gold medal in Bordeaux in 1990. *Vins de cépage* are also made from Cabernet Sauvignon, Merlot, Grenache and Syrah, together with a small quantity of Sauvignon Blanc and Chardonnay.

There are a number of very picturesque hill villages in the countryside near Valvignères: St Montant, St Thomé, Alba-la-Romaine, Aubignas and Rochemaure – beside the Rhône – are all well worth seeing.

The essential excursion here though is to the gorges of the Ardèche, the reach of the river between Vallon-Pont-d'Arc, so named because of the curious pinnacle of rock through which the river has tunnelled, and St Martin-d'Ardèche. The D 290 leads westwards from the N 86 a few kilometres to the north of Pont-St-Esprit and follows the left bank of the river. There are numerous breathtaking views from stopping-points situated along the route, and in some places you can walk down to the water's edge.

There are a number of smaller, but equally dramatic gorges in the region. From the town of Ruoms the D 4 crosses the Ardèche and leads north-west along the right bank for a few kilometres, offering quite staggering views as the river winds between steep, jagged cliffs. A short distance to the west of Ruoms is the small village of Labeaume, built in the gorges of the River Beaume.

About 10 kilometres south-west of Labeaume is a curious region of eroded limestone rocks called the Bois de Païolive. From Labeaume follow the D 208 through Chandolas, and a short distance to the south of Maison-Neuve on the D 104, a small road leads through this strange landscape to Les Vans. Don't miss seeing the ancient village of Naves, a few kilometres to the west. This little cluster of crumbling stone houses looks as if it has hardly changed at all for several hundred years.

The village of Balazuc is another sight worth seeing. Balanced on the edge of a sheer cliff above a bend in the Ardèche between Ruoms and Aubenas, a harmonious group of grey limestone houses, a fourteenth-century Romanesque church and the remains of ramparts create a memorable view. In medieval times the village was a stronghold for the silver-mine lords of neighbouring Largentière. This old walled village is also worthy of a visit. With its castle perched above and its fortified entrance gates, it retains a strong medieval ambience. Ten kilometres or so to the east is Vogüé, another impressive village on the banks of the Ardèche, with a row of old houses surmounted by a castle.

For those seeking a quiet and comfortable hotel, Le Chêne Vert, on a vine-covered hill in the hamlet of Rocher, to the north of Largentière, has much to commend it. An old-fashioned *auberge* with a modern extension, it offers a swimming pool and good country-style food.

COLLINES RHODANIENNES

In the north of the *département* of the Ardèche is the wine-growing region of St Joseph, which incorporates an area along the right bank of the Rhône between St Peray, outside Valence, and Chavany, about 60 kilometres to the north. The old riverside town of Tournon is the heart of this region, and the vineyards which are entitled to the St Joseph AOC appellation, granted in 1956, amount to about 500 hectares.

The medieval village of Balazuc perched on a cliff above the River Ardèche.

In addition to individual producers, there are also a number of Cave Co-opératives which, along with AOC St Joseph wines, also produce Vins de Pays des Collines Rhodaniennes. This newly-formed zonal appellation can apply to wines which originate from vineyards in an area of countryside which straddles the *départements* of Rhône, Drôme, Isère and Loire.

As a zonal Vins de Pays it is different from the confusingly-named Comtés Rhodaniens, a regional appellation which can include wines from the Coteaux de l'Ardèche, Coteaux des Baronnies, Comté de Grignan, Collines Rhodaniennes, Coteaux du Grésivaudan, Balmes Dauphinoises, Allobrogie and Urfé.

I visited the co-operative at Sarras, north of Tournon, during the harvest in late September, and there were long lines of tractor-drawn trucks waiting to disgorge their grapes into the winery. In just a few weeks the Vin Primeur, made from Gamay using carbonic maceration, would be on sale, and the fermentation vats were already bubbling away vigorously.

Primeurs are widely made in the Rhône valley, and since they are on sale on the third Thursday in October, they offer an opportunity to sample the new wine some weeks before the more widely marketed Beaujolais Nouveau is available at the end of November. (A Primeur is made on the premise that it will be consumed by Christmas, or thereabouts, while a Nouveau can be expected to remain sound for about one year after bottling.) The Sarras co-operative also make varietal Collines Rhodaniennes from Syrah, Marsanne and traditionally fermented Gamay – the three principal varieties of the region.

A few kilometres north of Sarras, the co-operative of St Desirat, which produces varieties of *vins de cépage* similar to those at Sarras, is also worth a visit. Both of these co-operatives are open on Sundays. The Cave Co-opérative at Le-Péage-de-Roussillon further to the north, also produces a Collines Rhodaniennes Chardonnay and a Merlot, together with a Cabernet Sauvignon rosé, in addition to Marsanne, Syrah and Gamay.

The town of Tain-l'Hermitage, set below a vine-

covered hill, lies on the opposite bank of the Rhône to Tournon. The co-operative here is renowned for its AOC Crozes Hermitage, but it also makes an excellent red Collines Rhodaniennes from Syrah, as well as a Gamay, a white wine from Marsanne and a Syrah rosé. These wines are produced from vineyards which fall outside the area delimited for AOC wines.

DRÔME

There's a sign on the A 7 Autoroute some distance to the south of Montélimar which announces, 'Vous Etes en Provence!' But the presence of the Mediterranean begins to make itself felt some time before this. The sparkling quality of the light, the warmth of the sun, the red-tiled houses, lavender fields, olive groves and pine-covered hillsides all combine to create the magical quality of Provence well before the official border is reached.

I've always felt that the valley of the Drôme is the true, geographical northern limit of Provence. It rises in the Haute Alpes de Provence and follows a winding, fast-running westward course to join the Rhône south of Valence. The little town of Die lies in the heart of the valley and is known for its Appellation Contrôlée wine, Clairette de Die, a sweetish sparkling wine made in a traditional way. A drier, *méthode champenoise* wine is also made, as well as still wines.

The vineyards extend along the valley of the Drôme, in some places planted high on the steep hillsides which border the valley. The greatest concentration is on the Drôme's great bend between the picturesque riverside town of Saillans and Luc-en-Diois, and around the village of Châtillon-en-Diois in the valley of the River Bez. The main villages of production are Aurel, Barsac, Saillans, Vercheny, Barnave, Châtillon, Menglon and St Roman.

The existence of Clairette de Die has been recorded as early as 77BC, when it was known as Aigleucos and unkindly described by Pliny the Elder as the least sophisticated wine of the Roman Empire. Laws were passed in 1380 to prevent any other wines being imported into the region.

Clairette de Die, which obtained its AOC title in 1942, is made from the grape variety of the same name and is also blended with Muscat to produce 'Clairette

Opposite: Vineyards of the Diois near the village of Saillans in the *département* of Drôme.

Orchards and vineyards near Vaison-la-Romaine in the *département* of Vaucluse.

Tradition' as well as a drier 'Brut' version. A number of other varieties are also grown to make the still wines which are allowed in the appellation.

The valley of the Drôme carves a deep swathe into an impressive mountain landscape and the countryside contains numerous picturesque villages and spell-binding vistas at every turn. From Die the D 518 leads along the valley of the Comane passing the pretty perched village of Chamaloc to the Col de Rousset, where a tortuously winding road provides stunning views of the Diois as it climbs to the summit.

Beyond is the Parc Régional du Vercors, a country-side of alpine-like meadows, racing rivers, gorges and craggy peaks. A round trip encompassing some of the loveliest corners of the Vercors can be made by following the road northwards to La Chapelle-en-Vercors and Villard-de-Lans, and returning via the Gorges de la Bourne to the pretty riverside town of St Jean-en-Royans. You can then drive south over the Sol de la Croix, and east to Vassieux-en-Vercors, before returning via the Col de Rousset to Die.

An enjoyable drive can be made into the countryside to the south-west of Die by following the Drôme downstream to Saillans, passing the village of Pontaix. This is built in a narrow defile, with old stone houses rising sheer from the river bank and a ruined château perched on the cliff above. From Saillans the D 156 climbs through impressive mountain scenery to the Col de la Chaudière before descending to the ancient town of Bourdeaux in the valley of the Roubion.

About 20 kilometres to the south-west, in the valley of the Jabron, is the medieval hilltop town of Le Poët-Laval, established in the twelfth century by the Hospitallers of St John of Jerusalem. Among the maze of steep cobbled streets is the ancient commander's residence, which has been converted into a comfort-able and atmospheric hotel with a good restaurant. A few kilometres to the north-west is Châteauneuf de Mazenc, another tiny community of crumbling stone houses on a hill overlooking the Jabron valley.

COMTÉ DE GRIGNAN

About 30 kilometres south-east of Montélimar is the village of Grignan, dominated by a massive eleventh-century fortress. The community was made famous in the seventeenth century by the writer Madame de Sévigné, who made frequent visits to her daughter, the Comtesse de Grignan.

The name is continued in a local Vin de Pays, Comté de Grignan, of which the largest producer is the Cellier de Dauphins in Tulette. Here they make both red and rosé wines from a blend of Grenache, Cinsault and Carignan, called the Cuvée de la Marquise de Sévigné. It is not possible to buy these wines directly from the *cave*, but they can be found in local shops and supermarkets.

Another producer of this small Vin de Pays is the Cave Co-opérative at St Maurice-sur-Eygues where, from about 7 hectares of vines, they make a Chardonnay and – a recent development – a Viognier.

In the Diois, the largest production of Vin de Pays de la Drôme is at the co-operative at Die, where a red wine is made from Gamay. It was formed in 1950 and has done a great deal to make the wines of the Drôme more widely known. The co-operative includes over 500 growers with over 600 hectares of vines and represents about 80% of the production. There are only a few independent wine-growers producing Vins de Pays.

One of these is Didier Cornillon, at St Romain, who makes a small quantity of a delicate rosé from a tiny plot of Gamay vines on the opposite side of the road to the vineyards from which he produces his Clairette de Die. His rosé has won several medals in recent years and sells out within a few months of being bottled.

Jacques Faures, whose vineyards border the Drôme around the village of Vercheny, near Saillans, produces rather more, making both red and rosé wines from about 1½ hectares of Gamay.

Beyond the Clairette de Die appellation zone, however, a considerable volume of Vin de Pays de la Drôme is produced from a much wider variety of grape types. The co-operative at St Gervais-sur-Roubion, to the east of Montélimar, is particularly interesting since it produces only Vins de Pays. The Merlot produced here was awarded a gold medal at the Paris Concours Général in 1992, and its Chardonnay received the same honour. It also produces a red Cabernet Sauvignon and Syrah, as well as a rosé from Cabernet Sauvignon and another from a blend based principally on Grenache and Cinsaut. An independent producer nearby, Jean-Pierre Forge at the Domaine de l'Orgeat near Monboucher-sur-Jabron, also makes an excellent Cabernet Sauvignon.

Among the other co-operatives who produce Vin de Pays de la Drôme are those at Beaumont-Montaux, to the north of Valence; at Loriol-sur-Drôme, to the south of Valence; at Viviers-sur-Rhône, south-west of Montélimar, and the Cave du Prieuré at Vinsobres, north of Vaison-la-Romaine.

COTEAUX DES BARONNIES

The little town of Nyons, built astride the River Eygues, is set in a crescent of mountains bordering the Tricastin plain which reaches away to the west. It has an arcaded square and a curious covered street leading to a gateway which was once the entrance to a castle. Nyons is the centre for another Vin de Pays within the *département* of the Drôme, called the Coteaux des Baronnies.

The majority of the production is by the co-operatives, the Union des Producteurs in Nyons and nearby Les Pilles, while a small quantity is produced at Vaison-la-Romaine, Puyméras and the Cave du Prieuré at Vinsobres.

The principal grape varieties for the reds and rosés are similar to those for the AOC Côtes du Rhône – Grenache, usually representing about 50%, with the balance of Cinsaut, Carignan and Syrah. Red wines of a single grape variety are also made from Syrah, Cabernet and Merlot, and a white wine from pure Chardonnay. There are a total of about 1,200 hectares farmed by nearly 500 *vignerons*.

The co-operative at Nyons is something of an Aladdin's cave for gourmets, since it also represents many of the region's olive producers. Here they make one of the finest cold-pressed virgin oils, and also sell the delectable Appellation d'Origine Contrôlée black olives harvested from a special variety, the Tanche, for which Nyons is famous. Other delights include grape-seed and walnut oil, honey, truffles, preserved fruits and jars of *tapénade*, the pungent Provençal paste made from olives, capers and anchovies.

The greatest concentration of vineyards lie along the valley of the River Eygues to the south-west of Nyons and around the villages of Buis-les-Baronnies,

Puyméras and Mirabel-aux-Baronnies.

One of the few independent producers of the Coteaux des Baronnies is Yves Liotaud, of the Domaine du Rieux Frais at Ste Jalle, a tiny community of old stone houses east of Nyons, beside the River Ennuye, a tributary of the Eygues.

M. Liotaud makes red wines from pure Syrah and Cabernet Sauvignon as well as a blended red from half-and-half Grenache and Syrah. A rosé is made from a blend of 70% Grenache and 30% Syrah, and a white from pure Chardonnay, which is kept for three to four months in oak barrels.

From Ste Jalle a scenic road climbs over the Col d'Ey and then descends into the valley of the Ouvèze. Here one can turn east on the D 546, which follows the river upstream through the most beautiful part of the steep-sided valley to a junction with the D 65. From here a detour can be made over the Col de Perty with spectacular views of mountainsides terraced with lavender fields before descending into the valley of the River Céans, a short distance along which is the very pretty medieval walled village of Orpierre.

Alternatively, at the foot of the Col d'Ey one can turn south on the D 546 to the little market town of Buis-les-Baronnies and then west along the valley of the Ouvèze towards Vaison-la-Romaine. Another very beautiful detour can be made a few kilometres after leaving Buis-les-Baronnies by taking the D 72 and following the valley of the Derbous before climbing over the Col de Fontaube and Col des Aires.

A few kilometres further east, beyond the little walled village of Reilhanette, is the Roman spa town of Montbrun-les-Bains with its houses tiered giddily up the side of a steep hill. It lies at the confluence of the Rivers Anary and Toulourenc and a pleasant way to return to Vaison-la-Romaine is to take the D 40 west along the valley of the Toulourenc, passing below the alarmingly perched village of Brantes, which is now partially deserted.

PRINCIPAUTÉ D'ORANGE

Between Vaison-la-Romaine and Orange, the Vin de Pays de la Principauté d'Orange is made by a number of independent producers as well as the Cave Co-opérative at Cairanne, which makes both red and rosé wines from a blend of 80% Grenache and 20% Carignan and a white from 75% Grenache Blanc and 25% Clairette.

Near the hamlet of Le Palis, a few kilometres west of Vaison-la-Romaine, a fruity and aromatic white wine is made by the Domaine St Claude from a blend of Chasan and Chardonnay, as well as a red from a blend of Grenache, Carignan and Counoise, an old grape variety used sometimes in the cocktail for Châteauneuf-du-Pape, and a rosé from Carignan and Grenache. Just 4 hectares are set aside for the Vins de Pays, while 30 are devoted to Côtes du Rhône.

VAUCLUSE

Vaison-la-Romaine is so named because of its extensive Roman ruins to the north of the modern town in the Puymin and Vilasse quarters. Remains of streets, houses, fountains and a theatre can be seen, as well as a large villa, but, sadly, parts of the remains were seriously damaged by the disastrous floods in the autumn of 1992.

The old village of Vaison-la-Romaine is set on a rocky hill above the left bank of the Ouvèze, which is spanned by a Roman bridge. It's an atmospheric web of cobbled streets, alleys and small squares decorated by fountains, around which are grouped old stone houses, some dating from the fourteenth century. From the ruins of a castle rebuilt in the fifteenth century there are extensive views of the surrounding countryside.

The town lies to the north of the Dentelles de Montmirail in the *département* of the Vaucluse. Vast areas of vines pattern the landscape from which both AOC Côtes du Rhône and Côtes du Ventoux are produced. To the south of the *département*, around the town of Apt, are the vineyards from which the Côtes du Lubéron are produced. The Vin de Pays du Vaucluse covers this entire area and is produced extensively by both Caves Co-opératives and independent producers, although most of the former are in the south.

The Domaine Durieu at Châteauneuf-du-Pape is one of a number of producers in the region who have planted Viognier, a variety associated with the northern Rhône, and are having considerable success with the white wine made from it, in addition to a red made from a blend of Grenache, Cinsaut and Syrah.

The *caveau* at the Domaine St Sauveur near Aubignan is situated in a charming eleventh-century chapel and produces both red and rosé wine from the local grape varieties of Grenache, Cinsaut, Syrah and

Above: A *pâtisserie* in the wine village of Lourmarin in the *département* of Vaucluse. Overleaf: Vineyards and lavender fields near the village of Gordes in the *département* of Vaucluse.

Carignan. The Domaine de Marotte near Carpentras produces another example of a successful, award-winning Viognier, as well as a white wine made exclusively from Roussanne.

The members of the co-operative at Apt have vineyards mainly in the Ventoux, with about 15% in the Lubéron, beyond the River Cavalon. In addition to red and rosé wines made from a blend of Grenache, Carignan, Cinsaut and Syrah, they also produce a Sauvignon Blanc and, since 1992, a Chardonnay. Other co-operatives producing Vin de Pays include those at La Tour-d'Aigues, Bonnieux, Cadenet, Cucuron and Lourmarin.

The importance of wine in this region is underlined by the presence of the university of wine at Suze-la-Rousse, east of Bollène, housed in a magnificent feudal castle which rises above the village rooftops. One of the prettiest and most popular villages in Provence, Séguret, lies at the foot of the Dentelles de Montmirail, a mountain with a distinctive cockscomb ridge.

A scenic road encircles the massif leading to the wine villages of Gigondas, Vacqueras and Beaumes-de-Venise. Don't miss the tiny fortified village of Le Barroux with its massive castle and a good hôtel-restaurant, Les Géraniums.

The road across the Dentelles de Montmirail from Beaumes-de-Venise to Malaucène is well worth a detour, and from Malaucène another road leads to the summit of Mont Ventoux, from which there are views as far as the mouth of the Rhône delta and the mountains of the Ardèche.

To the south, the countryside of the Lubéron is quintessential Provence, with plantations of sunflowers, lavender, fruit trees and the ubiquitous olive tree, and steep hillsides covered in pines, brush and wild herbs. It not only looks the way you imagine Provence to be, but also smells like it. Wine has been produced here since Roman times, although the vineyards have never had the same significance as those planted on the more northerly Rhône plain.

There is much to see of interest in the Lubéron, including a twelfth-century castle at Lourmarin and a fine Renaissance château at La Tour-d'Aigues. There is a ninth-century château at Ansouis, and a medieval castle at Mirabeau which was used as a location for the film of Marcel Pagnol's *Manon des Sources*.

The region is particularly rich in picturesque hill villages, notably Bonnieux, with two churches and a museum of bakery, Roussillon, with ochre houses rising from a sheer sandstone cliff, the artist's village of Gordes, the ancient village of Menerbes, and Lacoste, which is dominated by the château of the Marquis de Sade. There are oil mills at Cucuron and Oppède, and a lavender distillery which can be visited at Lagarde d'Apt.

Some of the best markets in Provence are held in this region: at Apt on Saturdays, Pertuis on Fridays, Cavaillon on Mondays, Gordes on Tuesdays and, perhaps the best of all, at L'Isle-sur-la-Sorgue on Sundays.

BOUCHES-DU-RHÔNE

The River Durance flows to the south of the Montagne du Lubéron towards its confluence with the Rhône, and marks the northern border of the *département* of Bouches-du-Rhône. The wine-growing region is focused on the left bank of the Durance, in the countryside around the towns of St Rémy and Les Baux-de-Provence, the environs of Aix-en-Provence, the Etang de Berre and Montagne Ste Victoire. The AOC wines of the *département* are the Coteaux d'Aix en Provence, Les Baux, Côtes de Provence, in the east of the *département*, and the tiny appellations of Cassis and Palette.

Although punctuated by mountains, the landscape here is largely open and exposed to the Mistral, with distinctive walls of poplar and plane trees grown to protect the crops. In addition to vineyards there are extensive orchards from which the region's speciality of preserved fruits is produced. Here too the delicious Calissons d'Aix are made – diamond shaped candies made from preserved fruit, sugar and almonds.

The Vin de Pays des Bouches-du-Rhône covers all of this region and is extensively produced by the co-operatives as well as a number of independent

Left: A street in the village of Roussillon in the département *of Vaucluse.*

producers. The main grape varieties used are common to most of the southern Rhône valley: Cinsaut, Carignan, Syrah, Mourvèdre and Cabernet for the reds and rosés – which account for the majority of production; Ugni Blanc, Clairette and Sauvignon for the whites.

At the co-operative of Les Vignerons du Roy René at Lambesc, however, they have experimented with a new grape variety, the Caladoc, for their red and rosé wines. This is a cross between Grenache and Malbec, and they say that it suits their terrain very well, producing a well-balanced red wine with an intense purple robe and a bouquet of red fruits. They also produce a pure Syrah and a Cabernet Sauvignon, together with a blended red and rosé.

Among the other co-operatives which produce Vin de Pays are those at Eguilles, Auriol-la-Destrousse, La Fare-les-Oliviers, Pélissanne, Puyloubier, St Cannat, Trets and Velaux.

I also visited the Château de Fonscolombe, near Le Puy-Ste-Réparade, where they make an excellent Chardonnay. Out of a total of 200 hectares, from which their AOC Coteaux d'Aix en Provence is produced, 30% is given over to producing Vins de Pays.

The associated vineyard of Domaine de Boulléry has also had recent success with a Chardonnay produced from 3 hectares planted in 1989, with the first bottling ready for 1993. They also plan to try more unblended wines from the Muscat, Viognier and Merlot varieties. Blended reds and rosés are also made from Carignan, Cinsaut, Counoise (also known as Auban) and Grenache; a white is blended principally from Clairette, Ugni Blanc and a small percentage of Grenache Blanc and Sauvignon.

PETITE CRAU

There is another small Vin de Pays within the *département* of Bouches-du-Rhône called Petite Crau. It is produced by a single Cave Co-opérative at Noves, 10 kilometres south-east of Avignon. About 80 hectares of vines are grown on the slopes of the countryside called La Petite Crau to the south of the town, along with fruit trees, tomatoes and lettuces. This is a very different landscape to the Plaine de la Crau, a bleak, table-flat landscape of stony scrubland which lies further south between the Rhône estuary and the Etang de Berre.

The co-operative produces blended red and rosés called 'Cuvée des Amours' from Grenache, Carignan,

Merlot, Syrah and Cabernet Sauvignon, and whites from Ugni Blanc and Clairette with a small percentage of Grenache Blanc. They also produce a red called 'Cuvée Laures de Noves' from a blend of Syrah and Cabernet Sauvignon.

The old city of Aix-en-Provence is the heart and soul of the region and worthy of an extended visit. It was the capital of Provence until the Revolution and has a wealth of fine old buildings, a lovely cathedral, elegant squares, tree-lined avenues and ornate fountains. A stroll down the Cours Mirabeau under the soaring plane trees, or a lazy hour at a pavement café table from which you can watch the world go by, seems to encapsulate the essence of Provençal life. The little town of St Rémy-de-Provence, to the south, is equally charming on a smaller scale and has one of the prettiest country markets in its small square each Saturday.

A few kilometres further south, the village of Les Baux-de-Provence is not to be missed. Once the stronghold of the feudal lords of Les Baux, of whom Raymond de Turenne was the most notorious, the village controlled a large part of the south of France. The fortifications were finally dismantled by Louis XIII in 1663. The substantial remains, known as the Ville Morte, are ranged along a lofty ridge, and are a very atmospheric place which still evokes the feeling of power the inhabitants once held. As the wind whips over the sun-bleached stone walls, and one gazes at the view extending for miles across the sweeping plain, it's easy to imagine how impregnable they once thought themselves to be.

VAR

To the east of Marseilles, the Massif de Ste Baume marks the beginning of the *département* of the Var. This is the region of the AOC Côtes de Provence, although a small area to the south of Aix in the Bouches-du-Rhône is also designated. The VDQS wines of the Coteaux Varois are also produced here, as well as four different Vins de Pays.

The 'departmental' Vin de Pays du Var covers the entire wine-growing region of the Var and is very widely made by both co-operatives and independent producers. Vin de Pays de la Maure is an appellation reserved for the vineyards south of the River Argens

Opposite: A Provençal farmhouse near the village of Lorgues in the *département* of Var.

A landscape near the village of Roquebrune-sur-Argens in the *département* of Var.

on the Monts des Maures, between St Raphael and Toulon. Vin de Pays d'Argens is reserved for those with vineyards around the valley of the Argens but, in practice, most growers and co-operatives prefer to use the more widely known names of Var or Maures.

At the Domaine Les Clairettes, near Les Arcs-sur-Argens, red and rosé Vin de Pays d'Argens are produced from Cinsaut, Grenache and Mourvèdre. The prestigious winery of Castel Roubine, between Lorgues and Draguignan, is best known for its Cru Classé Côtes de Provence, but it also makes a small quantity of Vin de Pays d'Argens. They use a similar blend of regional grape varieties to those used for their Côtes de Provence, growing them on hillsides surrounded by pine and oak forests. They also produce a blended white wine based on Clairette, Ugni Blanc and Semillon, varietal red and rosé wines from Cabernet Sauvignon, as well as a Chardonnay under the banner of Vin de Pays du Var.

MONT-CAUME

A similar blurring of titles applies also to the Vin de Pays du Mont-Caume, which is produced in the vineyards on the coastal plain between Bandol and La Ciotat. The first traces of vineyards here date from 600 BC, and the Romans were great admirers of the wines of Bandol. It is claimed there are 3,000 hours of sun here each year to ripen the grapes, and the local *vignerons* say their wines benefit from the unique mixture of sun, sea and Mistral.

Although the majority of the independent producers choose to use the title Vin de Pays du Var, the co-operatives here have opted to use their own appellation. Just outside the attractive old hill village of La Cadière-d'Azur, the *vignerons* of La Cadièrenne produce Vin de Pays du Mont-Caume alongside their AOC Bandol and Côtes de Provence.

The red wines are considered to be the glory of the region, the Mourvèdre being the dominant grape

A vineyard in the Massif des Maures near the village of Plan-de-la-Tour in the *département* of Var.

variety, and the co-operative uses a blend which also includes Cinsaut and Grenache. Their white wine is produced from a blend of Clairette and Ugni Blanc. The co-operative at St Cyr-sur-Mer also produces Vin de Pays.

At the Domaine la Roche Redonne, which has about 8 hectares of vines on the slopes below the village of La Cadière-d'Azur, they make both red and rosé Vin de Pays du Mont-Caume from the vines which have not reached the necessary maturity of eight years' growth to be used for their AOC Bandol. A blend of Mourvèdre, Cinsaut, Grenache and Carignan is used, and in 1992 for the first time a white wine was produced from just 1 hectare of Clairette.

One of the most interesting producers of Vin de Pays du Var is the Domaine de Triennes near Nans-les-Pins, under the shadow of the Massif de Ste Baume. Although the vineyards lie within the area designated for the VDQS appellation of Coteaux Varois, they choose to make only Vin de Pays as they do not have the necessary Grenache and have no wish to plant it.

They have had considerable success with a number of the wines produced here. 'Les Aurélien' made from Cabernet Sauvignon and Syrah, is kept in oak casks for 15 months, while a Chardonnay, with just 5% Ugni Blanc added for the acidity, is kept for 8 months. A beautifully delicate Vin Gris is made from pure Cinsaut by the *saignée* method, allowing skin contact for just two to three hours, and a Blanc de Blancs is also made from pure Ugni Blanc. The estate of 50 hectares was taken over in 1990 and revitalized by three friends – two wine-makers from Burgundy and a Parisian businessman.

I was interested to meet an independent producer of Coteaux Varois, the appellation they rejected, and a colleague in nearby St Maximin was recommended, the Domaine du Deffends. It is in a remote spot a few kilometres to the west of the town, hidden by a ring of low hills covered in pines at the foot of the Aurélien range.

The Domaine's *pièce de résistance* is the 'Clos de la Truffière' named after the truffles which can be found growing around the vines. It is made principally from Cabernet Sauvignon and Syrah for body, flavour and colour, with a small percentage of Grenache and Cinsaut added for fruitiness, bouquet and suppleness. They are vinified separately, and the balance of the blend is varied each year according to conditions. A pale 'Rosé d'une Nuit' is also made from Cinsaut with a smaller percentage of Grenache.

LES MAURES

The Massif des Maures rises from the coastline between St Raphaël and Hyères, a landscape of deep narrow valleys and steep slopes covered in pines, oaks and chestnut trees. Beginning at Roquebrune-sur-Argens just west of Fréjus, a splendid scenic tour can be made by following the mountain road to the villages of Plan-de-la-Tour, La Garde-Freinet, Grimaud and Collobrières, the chestnut centre of the Massif des Maures and famous for its *marrons glacés*.

From here a road leads over the Col de Babaou to join the coast at Bormes-les-Mimosas, and the circuit can be completed by following the coast road to Canadel-sur-Mer and then taking the road over the Col du Canadel, from which there are spectacular views of the coastline, before returning via Cogolin.

This attractive little town is best known for its production of smokers' pipes but, like many of the villages in the Maures, it also has a Cave Co-opérative producing a variety of Vins de Pays. These include a deep-robed dry rosé made from the Tibourin, a traditional variety of the region with a distinctively Provençal bouquet of the *garrigue* which is especially suited to making full-bodied rosés. A pure Merlot is also made here as a Vin de Pays du Var.

An interesting independent producer of Vin de Pays des Maures is the Château d'Astros, just north-west of Vidauban. The history of the *domaine* can be traced back to the twelfth century when its existence was recorded by the Knights Templars. Today it has 44 hectares of vines, of which only 20% is used to produce Côtes de Provence, the remainder being devoted to Vin de Pays. A novel aspect of the château's enterprise is a scheme for picking your own apples for winter storage – perhaps in the same cellar as your wines.

The wines produced here include reds from Grenache, Carignan and Cabernet Sauvignon, rosés from Grenache Cinsaut and Carignan, and whites from Ugni Blanc and Sauvignon. A rosé is also produced from pure Cinsaut, as well as a red Cabernet Sauvignon which is aged in wood.

An enjoyable circuit of this northern part of the Var can be made by following the road from Les Arcs, where there is a very pretty medieval village perched on a hill above the modern town, to a sequence of villages starting with Flayosc and Lorgues, both typically Provençal with squares shaded by plane trees, rippling fountains and tall mellow houses with shuttered windows.

Near Le Thoronet is a twelfth-century abbey, a fine example of Romanesque architecture built by the Cistercians. To the south of Carcès is a lovely artificial lake popular in summer for picnicking and watersports. Don't miss the little village of Entrecasteaux, hidden in a wooded valley with an eleventh-century château and gardens designed by Le Nôtre. The village is locally renowned for both its wines and its excellent olive oil.

To the west is the little town of Cotignac, set at the foot of a sheer cliff. It has a long sloping main street lined with plane trees, under which you can sit at a pavement café and absorb the atmosphere of Provence.

A few kilometres north of Entrecasteaux is the wine village of Villecroze, set high on the mountainside with sweeping views. Nearby is the charming little village of Tourtour, which you enter by gateways to find a lovely small square shaded by two enormous elm trees which are over 350 years old.

The delightful little hilltop village of Fox-Amphoux, 10 kilometres north-west of Cotignac, is well worth a visit to savour its old houses and quiet streets as well as a stunning view over the surrounding countryside. There's a charming hotel here, Le Vieux Fox, set in the ancient presbytery beside the church.

Many of these villages have a Cave Co-opérative as well as independent producers inviting a visit along the way, so there are frequent opportunities to sample and buy wine.

COTEAUX DE PIERREVERT

Near Manosque, just north of the confluence of the Rivers Durance and Verdon, is the little walled town of Pierrevert. It lies at the eastern edge of the Montagne du Lubéron, just within the *département* of Alpes-de-Haute-Provence, and gives its name to a small wine-growing region with a VDQS appellation acquired in 1959, Coteaux de Pierrevert.

There are about 400 hectares of vines farmed by nearly 300 *vignerons* in the countryside around the towns of Pierrevert, Manosque, Villeneuve, Gréoux-les-Bains and Quinson. Geographically the vineyards can be considered to be an extension of those in the north-east of the Vaucluse and the north-west of the Var, but the wines are quite different.

The main production is by the co-operatives at Pierrevert and their allied *caves* at Villeneuve and Quinson. At present the co-operative at Manosque is independent, but there are moves afoot for an amalgamation. At the Pierrevert co-operative the red wines are made from a blend of 50% Grenache, 20% Cinsaut and Syrah and 10% made up of Carignan, Auban and Mourvèdre; rosé wines are made using 60% Grenache, 30% Cinsaut and 10% Syrah; the white wine from a blend of Ugni Blanc, Grenache Blanc and Clairette.

ALPES-DE-HAUTE-PROVENCE

The *cave* also produces the 'departmental' Vin de Pays des Alpes-de-Haute-Provence, which is essentially produced from the excess of 50,000 hectolitres per hectare permitted for the Coteaux de Pierrevert. In addition to the blended wines it produces two varietal wines, not permitted in the VDQS appellation, a Cabernet Sauvignon and a Chardonnay.

There are, in addition to the co-operatives, a number of independent producers of whom the largest is the Domaine de Regusse, with a massive 230 hectares of vines representing no fewer than 17 varieties. The vineyard is planted in the *garrigue* a few kilometres south-west of Pierrevert on the road to La Bastide-des-Jourdans.

This very large vineyard has been established since 1971 in a region in which vines had not previously been planted. As well as Coteaux de Pierrevert and Côtes du Lubéron, the *domaine* produces a wide range of varietal Vins de Pays, from Syrah, Pinot Noir, Cabernet Sauvignon, Gamay, Aligoté, Muscat Blanc and Viognier, together with a Chardonnay which is aged in wood.

The little stone village of Lurs, 10 kilometres north of Villeneuve, is perched on a steep domed hill overlooking the Durance valley, and well worth a visit. An

The lower gorges of the River Verdon near Quinson in the *département* of Alpes-de-Haute-Provence.

important stronghold in the Middle Ages, it belonged to the bishops of Sisteron who held the title of Princes of Lurs.

After falling into ruins at the end of the nineteenth century, the village was rediscovered by Maximilian Vox, the author of a classification of printer's typefaces, and was gradually restored and repopulated. A fortified gateway beneath a clocktower leads to streets which meander between ancient stone houses covered in summer flowers and creepers. The village is the venue for an annual conference of graphic artists.

The vineyards of the Alpes-de-Haute-Provence extend as far eastwards as Quinson, which is set in the lower gorges of the River Verdon. For those who appreciate dramatic scenery it's a region not to be missed. A road runs around the edge of the Lac de Ste Croix to the village of Moustiers-Ste-Marie, where the houses are tiered steeply up the sheer face of a towering twin-peaked mountain. A river rushes down between the two peaks, and a chain supporting a cross is suspended between them above the village. This was the result of a pledge made by a knight departing for the crusades.

At the east end of the lake there are roads leading

along both sides of the upper Verdon gorges, with a sequence of breath-taking views. It is undeniably one of the great scenic sights of France, but best appreciated on weekdays and out of season, as the narrow winding roads carved from the mountainside are not designed for busy traffic.

HAUTES-ALPES

There is a further pocket of Provençal vineyards higher up the Durance valley to the south of Gap. As you drive north out of Sisteron along the N 85, look out for a sign saying Route des Fruits et Vins. This marks the beginning of a route along the D 948 and 942 through the villages of Ribiers, Laragne-Montéglin, Monêtier-Allemont, Tallard, Valserres and Espinasse.

It's lovely countryside, although there are few signs of vineyards to begin with. However, if you've ever wondered where all those French Golden Delicious apples originate, this valley is the answer. The valley floor and hillslopes are filled by a virtual sea of orchards, with the compact trees planted and pruned as neatly as oversized vines.

The vineyards are centred around the villages of Monêtier-Allemont, Tallard, Valserres and Espinasses, where there are small co-operatives which are responsible for the majority of production. They are not always open, especially out of the holiday season, but the wines can be found in local shops.

I visited one of the few independent producers, Louis Allemand, near Espinasses. His 15 hectares of vines are planted on the steep slopes of a very beautiful part of the Durance valley, where snow-capped peaks crowd the horizon. He makes a robust red wine from a variety called Mollard, with a little Gamay and Syrah added; his rosé is made from 50/50 Muscat Blanc and Cinsaut vinified together; and a white is produced from Muscat d'Ore and Petit Gris. He also makes *eau de vie* (a distilled spirit) from a variety of fruits, and during my visit his ancient puffing *alembique* was busy distilling a powerful brew of *marc*.

The route north to Gap can be continued by following the D 3 at the head of the valley to the Barrage de Serre-Ponçon, where there are impressive views over the man-made lake towards the high peaks of the Savoie.

Opposite: The Grand Canyon of the River Verdon near the Lac de Ste Croix in the *département* of Alpes-de-Haute-Provence.

SOUTHERN FRANCE

GARD

Opposite: The River Gardon near Alès. Above: Harvesting the grapes near St André-de-Roquepertuis in the valley of the River Cèze.

The *département* of the Gard is the most northerly of the Languedoc, bordered in the north by the Ardèche and in the east by the River Rhône and Provence, while to the west the Cevennes rise up on the horizon like dark shadows. The *département* takes its name from the River Gard, or Gardon as it is also known. In fact, two rivers, both named Gardon, flow eastwards from the Cevennes, one through Alès and the other through Anduze, having previously been joined by a third, to merge before joining the Rhône between Avignon and Arles.

Just before its confluence with the Rhône, the Gard is spanned by the most remarkable aqueduct in Europe, the Pont du Gard, a magnificent three-storey construction with tiers of elegant arches. It was built in 19BC by Agrippa, the son-in-law of Augustus, to divert water from the River Eure near Uzès across the Gard to the Roman city of Nîmes. It fell into disuse

SOUTHERN FRANCE

GARD & HERAULT

km
ml

VALLERAUGUE

LE VIGAN

ALZON

Pégairolles-de-l'Escalette

ST GUILHEM-LE-DESERT

LODEVE

St Jean-de-la-Blaquière

St Jean-de-Fos

le Bousquet-d'Orb

le Mas-Delon

Montpeyroux

Aniane

ST-GERVAIS

BEDARIEUX

Octon

Gignac

CLERMONT

LA-SALVETAT-S-AGOUT

Hérépian

Aspiran

Paulhan

OLARGUES

Gabian

Adissan

ORB

Laurens

Caux

Villeveyrac

ST-PONS

Coujan

Roujan

Montagnac

Murviel-lès-Béziers

Pézenas

Cessenon-s-Orb

MEZE

ST-CHINIAN

Cazedarnes

Abeilhan

Cébazan

Servian

St Thibéry

Pinet

Montblanc

MINERVE

Puisserguier

HERAULT

la Livinière

Montouliers

Béziers

AGDE

Capestang

Cers

Olonzac

Nissan-lez-Ensérune

LE CAP-D'AGDE

VALRAS

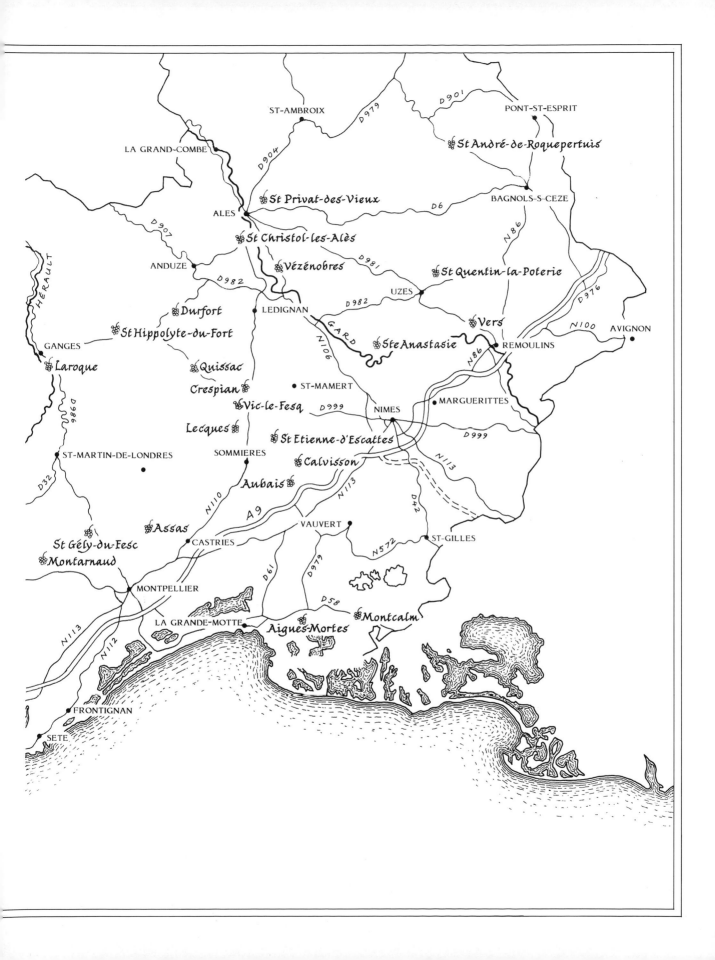

in the tenth century, and the structure was plundered for its stone, but in the nineteenth century it was restored by Napoleon III.

It's an immensely popular site and the best way to see it, especially in the summer, is to get there early, when the golden stone is lit by morning sunlight and before the convoys of coaches begin to arrive.

COTEAUX DU PONT-DU-GARD

The bridge gives its name to a Vin de Pays, Coteaux du Pont-du-Gard, which is produced by a group of seven Caves Co-opératives vinifying the grapes from a total of 1,000 hectares of vines. There are also about ten independent growers. The co-operatives' *caveau* is near the charming stone village of Vers, not far from the quarry where the stones used to built the Pont du Gard were hewn.

Here they produce a basic red wine blended from Grenache, Carignan and Syrah, a rosé using Grenache, Cinsaut and Carignan, and a white from Ugni Blanc, Clairette, Bourboulenc and Grenache Blanc. In addition, they make *vins de cépage* from Merlot, Chardonnay and Sauvignon Blanc.

Just to the south-east, the attractive old village of Castillon-du-Gard is built on a knoll, rising like a small island amid a sea of vines. The nearby town of Remoulins is famous for its cherries, and in the springtime a stunning display of blossom appears among the vineyards.

A few kilometres east of Vers is the ancient stone village of St Hilaire-d'Ozilhan, where the Hôtel-restaurant de l'Arceau offers comfortable accommodation and excellent cuisine in a lovely eighteenth-century house. To the west of Vers, in the heart of the gorges of the Gard at Collias, the Auberge le Gardon offers simple accommodation and good food and has a terrace overlooking the river.

COTEAUX DE CÈZE

Forty kilometres or so to the north of the Gard, the River Cèze follows a parallel course towards its confluence with the Rhône near Bagnols-sur-Cèze. This is an important production area for AOC Côtes du Rhône, with famous wine villages such as Chusclan, Laudun, St Victor-la-Coste, Lirac and Tavel. However, the region also has a Vin de Pays appellation, Coteaux de Cèze.

Many of these wines are sold *en vrac*, in bulk to

négociants or marketed as Vins de Pays du Gard, but the co-operative at St André-de-Roquepertuis offers an interesting selection of Coteaux de Cèze in addition to AOC Côtes du Rhône. A traditional red is produced here with 60% Grenache and a balance of Carignan and Cinsaut, and they also make *vins de cépage* from both Merlot and Cabernet Sauvignon. I had the opportunity to taste a wine made from the first harvest of a more recently planted 6 hectares of Chardonnay which, a few months before it was due to be bottled, tasted very promising.

The co-operative at St Alexandre, a few kilometres to the south of Pont-St-Esprit, also sells Coteaux de Cèze in bottles, with red, white and rosé wines blended from the usual traditional varieties, together with a keenly-priced Cabernet Sauvignon.

The valley of the Cèze is well worth exploring, with a maze of narrow lanes leading through unspoiled countryside to a sequence of picturesque villages. La Roque-sur-Cèze is especially pretty, built on a rounded hill which rises above the surrounding vineyards, its network of narrow cobbled streets leading up to a Romanesque chapel and the remains of a château.

Nearby is the Cascade du Sautadet, where the Cèze flows down over a series of saucer-like rocky depressions. The neighbouring village of Cornillon is perched high on a cliff-like bluff with far-reaching views of the valley, and the twelfth-century Chartreuse de Valbonne lies hidden in a peaceful wooded valley a few kilometres to the north-east.

About 20 kilometres to the south-west of the Cèze valley as the crow flies, the peak of Mont Bouquet creates a dramatic shape on the skyline. A small road leads up to the summit, from where there are breathtaking views of the *garrigue*, the Rhône valley, the mountains of the Ardèche and the Cevennes.

The mountain gives its name to a Vin de Pays grown in the vineyards planted on its slopes, Vin de Pays du Mont-Bouquet. The principal producer is the Cave Co-opérative at Brouzet-lès-Alès, but there is no *caveau*. Mont Bouquet is a name which seems destined to disappear under the mantle of Vins de Pays du Gard or des Cevennes.

The only independent producer I was able to trace is the domaine of La Grande Olivette at Moussan with

---

Opposite: The Pont du Gard near Remoulins. Overleaf: The view from the summit of Mont Bouquet near Alès.

a vineyard of 20 hectares or so. Only a small proportion of the grapes are vinified at the domaine, however, the remainder going to the local co-operative, which produces Vins de Pays du Gard.

The medieval town of Uzès is a short drive to the south of the Cèze valley. It has a wealth of fine old buildings and towers, some of which are currently undergoing extensive restoration. The main square, Place aux Herbes, is the location of a lively country market on Saturday mornings which, in the winter months, includes the stalls of truffle dealers. The impressive Ducal Palace is now the location of a sound-and-vision exhibition of the region's history.

DUCHÉ D'UZÈS

In the countryside around the town there are extensive vineyards which are used to produce Vin de Pays. They have a sound history, dating back over 2,000 years and gaining fame and honour by supplying wines to the popes of Avignon in the fourteenth century.

Recent changes have resulted in two new appellations, Duché d'Uzès and Cevennes. The former refers only to wines produced in the vicinity of Uzès, but the latter name can also include wines produced in Mont-Bouquet, Coteaux du Salavès and Libac, together with those of the former Uzège and Coteaux Cévenols appellations. In practice, Vins de Pays des Cevennes will probably mean the end of Mont-Bouquet and Coteaux du Salavès, while Libac has already disappeared.

The change is not simply a matter of name. The regulations too have been altered. The Cave Co-opérative at St Quentin-la-Poterie, a few kilometres northeast of Uzès, was one of the main production centres of Vin de Pays de l'Uzège, and their premium wine, 'Marquise des Terres Rouges', is made from a blend of Grenache, Syrah and Merlot. But the regulations for the newly-forged Duché d'Uzès do not allow the use of Merlot, so this particular wine has now become Vin de Pays des Cevennes, while their red and rosé wines made from Syrah and Grenache alone have become Vins de Pays de la Duché d'Uzès.

CEVENNES

The Domaine de Gournier, near the village of Ste Anastasie about 15 kilometres to the south-west of Uzès, has also suffered from the change in regulations, and has been obliged to change the name of its highly-regarded Vin de Pays de l'Uzège to Vin de Pays des Cevennes.

From a vineyard of 55 hectares the domaine produces varietal Chardonnay and Sauvignon together with a white wine blended from Ugni Blanc, Chasan and Rolle. A rosé is made from Grenache, Cinsaut and Mourvèdre, and a red wine from a cocktail of Merlot, Cabernet Sauvignon, Grenache, Syrah and Mourvèdre. There is also a superior red wine, made from Merlot and Cabernet Sauvignon, which is kept in oak for eight months before bottling.

The Domaine de Mallaigue, on the southern outskirts of Uzès, has a similar dilemma, as a significant proportion of the 45-hectare vineyard is planted with Merlot, which is used in conjunction with Cabernet Sauvignon to make a very successful non-traditional red in addition to a blended *rouge de pays*. M. Jean-Claude Reboul also makes a rosé from Grenache, Syrah and Cinsaut and a white wine from 100% Ugni Blanc.

Vin de Pays des Cevennes is also made at the Caves Co-opératives of St Christol-lès-Alès, Quissac and St Privat-des-Vieux in the suburbs of Alès. The *caveau* at the last sells red *vins de cépage* from Merlot and Cabernet Sauvignon and a Syrah rosé, and also contains a tempting selection of locally produced pâtés, olives, preserved fruits and jams, etc.

CÔTES DU VIDOURLE

To the south-west of Nîmes is the beautiful valley of the River Vidourle, with a succession of charming villages and towns along its banks. The river gives its name to Vin de Pays des Côtes du Vidourle, which is produced from the vineyards around the villages of Aspères, Crespian, Lecques, Souvignargues and Ville-vieille.

It's possible to buy wines directly from many of the smaller country Caves Co-opératives in the Languedoc, but not all have a *caveau* and some are open for sales to the public only once a week or less.

The well-run *caveau* at Crespian, however, is open during normal business hours, like most I have mentioned, and also represents the co-operatives of neighbouring Cannes and Montmirat. It has an excellent selection of Vins de Pays. A white Côtes du Vidourle is made here from a blend of Ugni Blanc, Sauvignon, Grenache Blanc and Rolle; a rosé, from Syrah, Cinsaut and Grenache, and a red wine from Syrah, Grenache and Carignan. *Vins de cépage* are also made with the

Vins de Pays d'Oc label from Sauvignon, Chardonnay, Merlot and Cabernet Sauvignon – red and rosé, the latter being an Hachette Guide selection for 1993.

I was only able to trace one independent producer of Côtes du Vidourle, M. Gérard Fabre at Clos de la Tourie in the attractive hilltop village of Aubais, a few kilometres south-east of Sommières. He farms 12 hectares or so of vines on the hillside near the village, making primarily red wines from Grenache, Syrah and Mourvèdre, but he has recently planted some Caradoc as well as Rolle, with which he will make some white wine in the future.

VAUNAGE

The Vaunage is a region immediately to the east of the Vidourle, near the charming old walled town of Sommières. In addition to producing AOC Costières de Nîmes, it gives its name to a Vin de Pays which is made from the vines grown here. The appellation is now largely disappearing under the Vin de Pays du Gard label, and the region's main Cave Co-opérative at St Côme gave up using the name a few years ago.

One notable upholder of the appellation, however, is M. Dominique Robin of the Domaine Mas de l'Escattes on the stony hillside a kilometre or so north-east of Calvisson. Here there are 40 hectares of vines, planted on three clearly defined types of terrain. Costières de Nîmes is produced on the well-drained alluvial soil of the steepest slopes; Coteaux du Languedoc on the higher, drier limestone *garrigue*; and the lowest slopes, planted with 15 hectares of vines, are ideal for the Chardonnay, Viognier and Cabernet Sauvignon grapes used for Vin de Pays.

The vineyards benefit from underground springs which gave the estate its name – it is derived from the Latin word *excatarire*, meaning to well up. In addition to varietal Vins de Pays, which include a Cinsaut rosé, M. Robin also makes a blended red wine from 50/50 Syrah and Grenache and a white from Chasselas with a small proportion of Chardonnay.

M. Henri Arnal, at the nearby village of Langlade, also produces Vin de Pays de la Vaunage but, unfortunately, I was unable to visit him.

COTEAUX DU SALAVÈS

The wine-growing region of this part of the Gard extends further up the valley of the Vidourle to the foothills of the Cevennes. The vineyards around the

A *charcuterie* in the village of St Paulet-de-Caisson in the *département* of Gard.

attractive villages of St Hippolyte-du-Fort, Durfort, Pompignan, Corconne and Quissac produce a Vin de Pays called Coteaux du Salavès. Sadly, it would seem that this long-established name is likely to disappear under the Cevennes banner as a number of Caves Co-opératives are beginning to change their labels.

The co-operative at St Hippolyte-du-Fort is appearing to resist the temptation, however, and still makes a red Coteaux du Salavès blended from Merlot, Cabernet Sauvignon, Syrah and Grenache and a white using Ugni Blanc, Clairette and Sauvignon. They also produce a Cevennes red using 80% Merlot and 20% Grenache, as well as a pure Sauvignon Blanc.

SABLES-DU-GOLFE-DU-LION

The most southerly vineyards of the Gard are planted on the bleak landscape of the Camargue. These can only be used to produce Vins de Pays with the name Sables-du-Golfe-du-Lion.

The vineyards planted here date back to the fourteenth century and have the distinction of being unique in France, in that the vines were not grafted on to American root stocks. This turned out to be unnecessary, as it was found that phylloxera could not survive on the sandy terrain. The area of production is mainly around the medieval walled town of Aigues-Mortes and Stes Maries-de-la-Mer, famous for its gypsy festival. It also extends westwards along the narrow coastal strip from the marina resorts of Le Grau-du-Roi and La Grande-Motte to Sète and Cap d'Agde in the *département* of Hérault.

The largest producer is Listel, but there are two smaller Caves Co-opératives based at Aigues-Mortes, as well as a number of independent producers. The Cave des Remparts makes a basic red wine from Cabernet Sauvignon and Carignan, and a Gris de Gris using Grenache Gris with a little Carignan and Merlot. A white wine is made from 100% Ugni Blanc, as well as a Chardonnay sold as Vin de Pays d'Oc.

The Cave Sabledoc can be found just east of Aigues-Mortes, along the road towards Stes Maries-de-la-Mer. Here they make a varietal Chardonnay and Sauvignon Blanc together with the region's speciality, Gris de Gris, and a basic blended red wine called Rouge Rubis.

Further along this road, near the village of Montcalm, is the Mas du Petit Pin, with its roadside 'Caveau du Chêne'. Here an excellent range of Vin des Sables is produced from a vineyard of 50 hectares. A Gris de Gris and a red wine are made here using Cabernet Sauvignon and Merlot, together with varietal white wines from both Chardonnay and Sauvignon Blanc.

One of the most highly-regarded independent producers of Vin des Sables is the Domaine du Petit Chaumont, with a vineyard of 114 hectares situated 3 kilometres from the sea between Aigues-Mortes and La Grande-Motte. Records have been discovered which mention the domaine's existence as early as the end of the thirteenth century.

Gris de Gris was responsible in the past for the domaine's main production and it is still of great importance, made here using Syrah, Grenache, Cinsaut, Merlot and Carignan. However, they also make a conventional rosé, from Cabernet Sauvignon, Merlot and Syrah, an excellent white wine, using a blend of 50% Sauvignon with 25% each of Chardonnay and Clairette, and a red wine from 50/50 Cabernet Sauvignon and Merlot.

Opposite: The village of Quissac on the banks of the River Vidourle in the *département* of Gard.

HÉRAULT

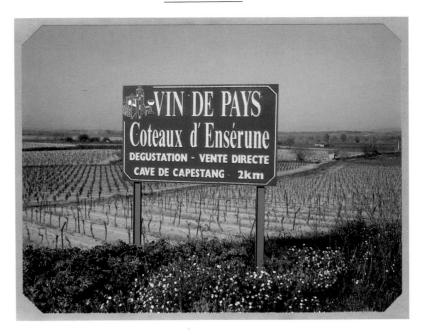

Opposite: The wine village of St Jean-de-Buèges in the *département* of Hérault. Above: The vineyards of the Coteaux d'Ensérune near Capestang in the *département* of Hérault.

The *département* of the Hérault, in the heart of the Languedoc, has been described as the world's largest vineyard. To even the most casual observer this would appear to be no exaggeration, since there are few corners of its landscape which are not planted with vines.

Quantity and quality are seldom completely compatible and, in the past, the Languedoc has had a reputation for the former at the cost of the latter. Things have changed a good deal in the past two decades, however, and some fine wines are now being produced in this region of France.

The introduction of new technology has played a large part in the improvement of Languedoc wines, and there are now many Caves Co-opératives and individual wine-makers who have made considerable investments in the very latest equipment and in the services of experienced oenologists.

Another factor which has played an important role in the development of new wines and fresh thinking is the change in the regulations controlling the region's viticulture which took place in 1966. The rules which forbade the use of non-traditional vines were relaxed, and wine-makers were allowed to introduce varieties from other regions, like Cabernet Sauvignon, Merlot and Chardonnay, into their vineyards.

COTEAUX DE MURVIEL

François Guy was the first *vigneron* in the region to plant the new varieties in 1967, and many people consider him to be very largely responsible for the new vitality and continuing quest for quality and innovation which have characterized the region's wine-making during the last three decades.

His domaine, Château Coujan, lies in an area of ideally exposed high ground a few kilometres north of the wine village of Murviel-lès-Béziers with its sixteenth-century château, to the north-west of Béziers. Here, over 100 hectares of vines are used to produce AOC Coteaux du Languedoc, St Chinian and Vin de Pays des Coteaux de Murviel.

M. Guy retired a few years ago and his daughter now looks after the domaine, but his enthusiasm and curiosity for new ideas are as strong as ever. 'I like to be original,' he told me. He produced a bottle of Vin de Table, a *vendange tardive* made from Petit Manseng grapes not picked until November because they had proved to be too acidic for his original purpose. As it had an alcohol potential of 18 degrees, well in excess of the regulatory limit, M. Guy was unable to label the wine Coteaux de Murviel.

Another recent 'originality' is a white wine made from Rolle, the variety grown in the small appellation of Bellet, near Nice, and also known as Vermentin in Corsica. He was told that his vineyard was not near enough to the sea for the variety to be successful, but he persevered until he found a clone which thrived on his terrain.

M. Guy also makes a rosé from Mourvèdre and another from Cabernet Sauvignon, as well as a Sauvignon Blanc and a red wine from a blend of 75% Merlot and 25% Cabernet Sauvignon, which is aged for two years in giant oak *foudres*, holding 200 hectolitres, before bottling.

He gave me the opportunity to taste the first wine that he bottled himself, in 1977 – superb. M. Guy had previously sold his wines in bulk to a *négociant*, but one year he felt the price offered was too low for the quality of his product and kept it instead. His new 'originality' for the coming years will be a red wine made from Pinot Noir vines which were planted in 1992.

Five generations of wine-makers have worked this domaine, which contains vines of over sixty years' maturity. The château is built on the site of a Roman villa and the vineyard contains a wealth of fossilized corals and shellfish, of which an impressive collection is dotted around the courtyard where doves and peacocks strut and flutter.

Château Coujan can be found by following a small road, the D 16E, which leads north from the D 16 at Murviel-lès-Béziers near the village's Cave Co-opérative. This establishment vinifies the grapes from a total of 1,300 hectares farmed by a large group of individual growers. The Vin de Pays des Coteaux du Murviel made here includes red varietal wines from Cabernet Sauvignon and Merlot together with a rosé made from 100% Cinsaut. With the Vins de Pays d'Oc label, the *cave* also produces an oak-aged Sauvignon Blanc and Cabernet Sauvignon together with a Syrah rosé and an un-oaked Sauvignon Blanc.

The AOC vineyards of the *département* of Hérault are included in the appellation Coteaux du Languedoc, and within this are a number of individual appellations such as St Chinian, Picpoul de Pinet, Clairette du Languedoc, Muscat de Frontignan and Fougères.

The Vins de Pays of the Hérault can be given the general, regional name of Oc, which means they can originate from vineyards anywhere within the Hérault, Gard, Aude or Pyrénées-Orientales, or they can be given the 'departmental' name of Vin de Pays de l'Hérault, which restricts their origins to that region. Alternatively they can be given the name of the zone of the production: the Hérault is divided into 28 separate areas, some of which are quite extensive, others restricted to the vineyards around a single village.

CESSENON

The Vin de Pays de Cessenon is one of these, the product of a small village in the valley of the River Orb a few kilometres to the west of Murviel-lès-Béziers. The village co-operative produces modestly-priced traditional wines from a total of around 200 hectares of vines, making a red from Syrah, Grenache, Carignan and Cinsaut, a rosé from mainly Grenache with a little Cinsaut, and a white from a blend of Maccabeo and Malvoisie.

The Orb is one of the loveliest rivers of the region and the road which leads north from Cessenon follows its winding course upstream, with a series of delightful views, to the picturesque villages of Roquebrun and Vieussan before joining the main road, the D 908.

HAUTE-VALLÉE DE L'ORB

A short distance to the west is the attractive old village of Olargues, set beside a meander of the River Jaur, which is spanned by stone bridge dating from 1202 known as the Pont du Diable (devil's bridge). To the east you come to the spa town of Lamalou-les-Bains and then Hérépian, famous for the Granier bell foundry which has produced bells for churches and cathedrals all over the world.

There is a Cave Co-opérative here, and another based in Le Bousquet-d'Orb further up the valley, which produce Vin de Pays de la Haute-Vallée de l'Orb. It's an extensive wine region, covering over 30 communes in the upper valley of the Orb, and produces only Vin de Pays. The emphasis here is on *vins de cépage*, and the *cave* at Bousquet-d'Orb makes excellent, and reasonably priced Chardonnay – they have over 100 hectares – Sauvignon Blanc, Merlot, Syrah and Cabernet Sauvignon.

The Cirque de Mourèze near the Lac du Salagou in the *département* of Hérault.

Don't miss seeing the small medieval walled village of Boussagues, a few kilometres south of Bousquet-d'Orb, with its ruined château and maze of narrow streets and alleys.

COTEAUX DU SALAGOU

To the east of Bousquet-d-Orb is the Lac du Salagou, a reservoir which was filled in 1958 and now covers 750 hectares. Surrounded by red rocks and *garrigue*, which in springtime is covered in masses of yellow broom and rockroses, the blue water makes a dramatic splash of colour and is a popular destination for picnickers, campers, fishermen and water-sports enthusiasts.

The hillsides around the lake are cultivated with vines which produce Vin de Pays des Coteaux du Salagou, and there is a Cave Co-opérative in the lakeside village of Octon. I visited Henri Delauge at the Domaine du Mas Delon near the hamlet of Le Puech, one of a few independent producers with a vineyard of 10 hectares. A white vine from 100% Grenache Blanc is made here, together with varietal rosés from Grenache and Syrah, a red from Syrah, and another blended red using Syrah, Grenache, Chenançon, Carignan and Cinsaut. M. Delauge is also known for his Cartagène, a fortified white wine based aperitif which is the Languedoc's version of the Charente's Pineau, Champagne's Ratafia and Gascony's Floc.

There is also a small Cave Co-opérative producing Coteaux du Salagou at Pégairolles-de-l'Escalette in the upper Orb valley to the north of Lodève. This very pretty little walled village is set amid dramatic scenery at the foot of the Causse du Larzac and is well worth visiting for its own sake.

A short distance to the south of the lake, the Cirque de Mourèze is a curious region of limestone outcrops eroded into fantastic shapes and distorted columns. Nearby is the village of Villeneuvette, which is approached by a splendid avenue of plane trees leading

to a monumental gateway. The community was set up in 1670 around a royal cloth-making factory with the support of Colbert, Louis XIV's finance minister.

MONT-BAUDILLE

To the east of the Lac du Salagou the landscape is dominated by the peak of Mont St Baudille, which rises to nearly 850 metres above sea level. The important wine villages of Montpeyroux and St Saturnin lie in its shadow, and along with AOC Coteaux du Languedoc the region also has a Vin de Pays appellation, Mont-Baudille, which is produced largely at the Cave Co-opérative of Montpeyroux. Most of the wine is sold in bulk to *négociants*, but they do also sell a red wine in what is called 'bag-in-a-box', a 10-litre collapsible container which will keep the wine in good condition for several months, even when half empty. This wine is blended from Cinsaut, Carignan and Syrah and is very inexpensive.

I visited one of the few independent producers, the Domaine d'Aupilhac, where Sylvian Fadat has 10 hectares of productive vines and 5 hectares newly planted near the village of St Saturnin. A red wine is made here using 100% Carignan from vines of 50 years' maturity, together with a white wine made from pure Ugni Blanc which was awarded a gold medal at the Languedoc wine fair in 1992.

At a local restaurant I tasted an excellent white Vin de Pays du Mont-Baudille which was made at Château Sauvageonne, near the pretty wine village of St Jean-de-la-Blaquière, but I was unable to meet the proprietor. The village is set in a beautiful valley below the massif of Mont St Baudille, where the distinctive red rock and soil of the region create a striking contrast with the neatly-planted rows of green vines.

You can drive to the summit of Mont St Baudille by following the D 9 from Montpeyroux north to Arboras, before climbing a winding pass from where there are breathtaking views on to the windswept limestone plateau.

GORGES DE L'HÉRAULT

To the east of Mont St Baudille the River Hérault winds its way through an impressive gorge near the picturesque village of St Guilhem-le-Désert. The com-

munity dates from the ninth century when Guillaume de Toulouse, a companion of Charlemagne, founded an abbey on the pilgrim route to Santiago de Compostela.

The vineyards in this region produce Vins de Pays des Gorges de l'Hérault, with the main production centred in the Caves Co-opératives of Gignac, Aniane and St Jean-de-Fos. At Aniane, basic red, white and rosé wines are made from blends of local varieties, together with a superior red made using just Syrah and Grenache. The *cave* of St Jean-de-Fos is known for its Sauvignon Blanc, and at Gignac a white wine is produced from a blend of Sauvignon and Ugni Blanc, together with a varietal Carignan and a Syrah rosé labelled Vin de Pays d'Oc.

A few kilometres to the north-west of St Guilhem-le-Désert, the little River Buèges runs a parallel course to the Hérault. It is one of the most beautiful valleys of the region, and the little stone village of St Jean-de-Buèges, with its ancient bridge and its château perched above, is a gem.

The small town of Aniane has a gourmet food boutique which contains one of the best selections of home-made preserves I've ever seen, together with a good range of local wines. For those seeking a comfortable hotel with excellent food at a reasonable price, I can happily recommend the Hostellerie St Benoît at Aniane, which also has a swimming pool.

On the *garrigue* to the east of the road between Aniane and Gignac is the Mas de Daumas Gassac, a domaine which has become renowned for its fine red wine, a Vin de Pays de l'Hérault which now commands prices more in line with the excellent clarets with which it is frequently compared. The neighbouring Château de Capillon has an outstanding local reputation for its Vins de Pays d'Oc, of which the Chardonnay is an excellent example.

VAL DE MONTFERRAND

The largest of all the Hérault's Vin de Pays regions, Val de Montferrand lies to the north-east of Gignac, covering about 50 communes between Ganges in the north and Montpellier in the south. Named after a ruined château at the foot of Pic St Loup, the wine is produced by a large number of Caves Co-opératives as well as a few independent producers.

The Cave Co-opérative of the village of Assas, for example, produces well-made and very modestly

Opposite: Vineyards near the wine village of St Jean-de-la-Blaquière.
Overleaf: The River Hérault at the village of St Guilhem-le-Désert.

priced wines. These include a red blended from Carignan, Cinsaut, Grenache, Cabernet Sauvignon and Merlot, a white using Terret Blanc and Grenache Blanc, and a rosé from mainly Syrah with just a little Grenache. Unusually, the co-operative also makes a Viognier, Domaine de Perret, which is also labelled Vin de Pays du Val de Montferrand.

At St Gély-du-Fesc the co-operative makes a pure Merlot, a Syrah rosé and a white from Ugni Blanc as well as a Chardonnay, while the most northerly co-operative, at Laroque, makes a red Cabernet Sauvignon. Laroque is a nice old town set beside a broad weir on the River Hérault, just south of Ganges. On a cliff above the town are the imposing remains of a silk factory built in the eighteenth century, with rows of elegant arched windows to provide light for the workers.

I visited the Domaine de Peuch in the village of St Clément-de-Riviére, an independent producer of Val de Montferrand. Varietal reds are made here from Cabernet Sauvignon and Merlot, together with a rosé using Cabernet Sauvignon and a white from pure Ugni Blanc. A Chardonnay is made with the Vin de Pays d'Oc label, and the domaine also produces an interesting aperitif, Vin d'Orange, a fortified white wine flavoured with oranges and spices.

BÉRANGE

To the south-east of the Val de Montferrand are the two small appellations of Bérange and Benovie, both of which appear to exist largely in name only. I visited the Château de Fontmagne where one of the few independent producers of Vin de Pays du Bérange farms 12 hectares of vines near Castries. A blended red is produced here using Grenache, Cinsaut and Syrah, together with a rosé, from Syrah and Grenache, which is also used to make a sparkling, *méthode champenoise* wine.

COLLINES DE LA MOURE

The Montagne de la Moure, to the south-west of Montpellier, is a *massif* rising to about 300 metres above sea level and overlooking the eastern edge of the Bassin de Thau. It gives its name to one of the larger production areas of Vins de Pays, Collines de la Moure, covering about 30 communes with the main production centred on the region's Caves Co-opératives. They tend to make blended wines from traditional

local varieties as well as *vins de cépage* from more recently introduced, classic varieties. At Montbazin, for example, the co-operative makes a Blanc de Blancs from Sauvignon and a red using 100% Merlot, while at Montarnaud a traditional red is made from a blend of Grenache, Carignan, Cinsaut, Syrah and Merlot.

Of the few independent producers, the Domaine de Terre Mégère at Cournonsec is notable for the production of a Viognier, a white wine variety which is encountered frequently in the Rhône region but is far less common in the Languedoc. An excellent Merlot is also made here. Another producer of Collines de la Moure is the vineyard of the twelfth-century Abbaye de Valmagne.

VICOMTÉ D'AUMELAS

Just north of the Montagne de la Moure is a region known as the Pays d'Aumelas, a limestone plateau which gives its name to a Vin de Pays, Vicomté d'Aumelas. With a vineyard area of 7,000 hectares, farmed by 2,600 individual members, the wines are produced by a group of Caves Co-opératives whose headquarters are at Plaissan. Red and rosé wines are made here, using a blend of Grenache, Syrah and Cinsaut, and a white using Carignan Blanc and Ugni Blanc.

CÔTES DU CÉRESSOU

Vin de Pays des Côtes du Céressou is produced in the region immediately to the west of the Pays d'Aumelas around the villages of Paulhan, Adissan and Aspiran in the valley of the Hérault. This area has its own AOC appellation, Clairette de Languedoc, a white wine made exclusively from the Clairette variety.

At the Aspiran co-operative a red Côtes du Céressou is produced from a blend of Carignan and Merlot, and a Gris de Gris from Grenache Gris with a little Clairette. The Paulhan co-operative makes a pure Carignan rosé, a red using a blend of Carignan, Grenache and Alicante, and a white from 100% Terret Bourret. The Terret variety is found chiefly in the Hérault, where it is quite widely planted, and it has the strange characteristic of being able to produce white, black and grey bunches of grapes on the same vine. To confuse matters further, Terret Blanc is also known as Bourret Blanc, and Terret Gris as Terret Bourret.

At Adissan, 50% each of Syrah and Grenache is used for the red and rosé wines, and a white is produced from Clairette, Terret Bourret and Grenache Blanc as well as a pure Sauvignon Blanc. If you have a suitable colour photograph, this last co-operative offers the novelty of personalized labels for a small extra charge. The service takes about a week, but is available even for just a dozen or so bottles and is very popular with local people for events like christenings – complete with a picture of the new baby on the label.

CAUX

To the south-west of the Côtes du Céressou, two villages and a château give their names to three small Vin de Pays appellations: Caux, Laurens, Cassan. The nearest to Adissan is Caux, a pretty cluster of stone houses dominated by a fortified church, and known primarily for its rosé.

Apart from a few individual growers, most of the production is by the Cave Co-opérative, with about 350 members farming a total of 1,000 hectares. The content of the wines varies from year to year, but in 1992 the *cave* made a rosé from 100% Grenache, a red using 50/50 Mourvèdre and Syrah, and a white wine from a blend of Chardonnay, Ugni Blanc and Terret Bourret.

I visited Maurice Calas, an independent producer with 23 hectares of vines planted on the slopes around the village. He makes a red wine from Merlot, Grenache, Carignan and Syrah, which are vinified separately before blending, and a rosé from the same group of varieties using juice from the first pressing with the addition of some Cinsaut. A large proportion of his vineyard has vines with at least 50 years' maturity.

CASSAN

Vin de Pays de Cassan is named after the Château de Cassan near the village of Gabian, about 8 kilometres west of Caux. Here the Cave Co-opérative, La Carignano, founded in 1936, makes an interesting range of Vins de Pays in addition to their AOC Coteaux du Languedoc.

A red wine is produced here from a blend of Cabernet Sauvignon and Merlot, as well as varietal reds from Syrah and Carignan, the latter using carbonic maceration. A Gris de Gris is made from Grenache Gris, and a Blanc de Blancs from a blend of Carignan Blanc and Terret Blanc. The co-operative at the neighbouring village of Roujan also produces Vin de Pays de Cassan.

Vineyards near Pézenas in the *département* of Hérault.

COTEAUX DE LAURENS

The village of Laurens, 22 kilometres north of Béziers, is dominated by a castle built in the twelfth century on a jagged spur of rock. After several transformations, and partial destruction during the Revolution, the restored building is now the town hall. The Cave Co-opérative of Laurens sells red Coteaux de Laurens only in bulk, and largely to *négociants*, but at the Caveau des Schistes, the co-operative's shop on the main road, one can buy a Vin de Pays in bottles – a Blanc de Blancs made from a blend of Carignan Blanc and Terret Blanc using low temperature fermentation.

PÉZENAS

Just south of the Côtes du Céressou is the charming old town of Pézenas. In the seventeenth century, this was the capital of the Languedoc and many fine buildings survive from this period. Pézenas is famous for its connection with Molière, who brought his company here many times to perform for the town's nobility and high society. The town's other claim to fame is Petits Pâtés de Pézenas – small crusty pies made from minced lamb which is sweetened and spiced.

Pézenas is also known for its Vin de Pays. There are a few independent producers, but the driving force behind the appellation is the Cave Co-opérative –

called Molière. In addition to red, white and rosé wines blended from the usual local varieties, the co-operative makes varietal wines, from Merlot and Sauvignon Blanc, with the latter also offered as an oak-aged variant. A superior blended red, 'Barbier Gely', is made from Syrah and Grenache and aged in oak casks for two years before bottling.

COTEAUX DE BESSILLES
The Coteaux de Bessilles area lies to the east of Pézenas around the small town of Montagnac. The appellation's Cave Co-opérative, Le Cellier de St André, is based in the town, vinifying the grapes produced from a vineyard area of about 2,500 hectares. A wide range of varietal Vins de Pays are made here, from Syrah, Grenache, Merlot, Cabernet Sauvignon and Mourvèdre. The last is also used to produce an oak-aged wine which has received considerable acclaim.

A light red wine called 'Cuvée Bicentenaire' is produced from Carignan, using carbonic maceration, while 'Cuvée du Cinquantenaire', is an oak-aged red wine made from Grenache and Syrah. The *cave* also produces white wine from Sauvignon Blanc, a quantity of which is matured in oak casks before bottling.

Of the half dozen or so independent producers of Coteaux de Bessilles, I visited the Domaine de la Vézenobre near Montagnac, where M. Christophe de Beauregard has a vineyard of 40 hectares. His wines include a Cabernet Sauvignon matured in oak casks for four months, a Grenache rosé and a Sauvignon Blanc.

CÔTES DE THAU
To the south-east of the Coteaux de Bessilles is the Bassin de Thau, a salt-water lake which is used extensively for the cultivation of shellfish. The lakeside towns of Mèze and Bouzigues are completely dominated by shops, kiosks and restaurants offering '*dégustations*'.

I stopped for lunch in Bouzigues at a small restaurant, Le Jardin de la Mer, built on a wooden platform above the sheds where the oysters and mussels are brought in by small boats to be sorted and graded. A mixed dish of raw oysters, mussels gratinéed with breadcrumbs, olive oil and garlic, together with giant

prawns grilled over the embers of a fire made with old vine stumps was, quite simply, the best shellfish I have ever tasted.

The local choice to accompany such a meal is Picpoul de Pinet, a dry white AOC wine dating back to Roman times. In 1618 it was cited as being one of the six most renowned wines of the Languedoc, and it is claimed that the Emperor Napoleon III chose Picpoul de Pinet to drink at the banquet celebrating his marriage. The region suffered a catastrophic hailstorm in the spring of 1991, and the harvest was only saved by the heroic efforts of 1,500 *vignerons* who had the task of re-pruning one and a half million vines within a few days.

Vin de Pays des Côtes de Thau is the Vin de Pays alternative made in this region and, like the Marches de Bretagne in the Muscadet region, was designed to allow a red wine to be made in an area whose prime appellation permits only white.

The Cave de l'Ormarine at Pinet makes a red wine blended from Merlot, Carignan and Grenache, and a rosé using Grenache and Syrah. A white Côtes de Thau is made for local consumption from a blend of Terret Bourret, Carignan Blanc and Grenache Blanc, together with a Blanc Moelleux called Domaine des Martin, using Terret Blanc and Sauvignon. The Cave Co-opérative at nearby Pomerols also makes excellent Vin de Pays as well as Picpoul de Pinet.

Claude Goujal, an independent producer at the Domaine de la Rouqette in the village of Pinet, makes varietal Merlot and Sauvignon Blanc from a total of 26 hectares. These are currently labelled Côtes de Thau, but he intends to adopt the Vin de Pays d'Oc appellation in the future, as it is so much more widely known outside the region.

CÔTES DE THONGUE
To the west, beyond the River Hérault, is the Côtes de Thongue, a thriving Vin de Pays appellation covering the vineyards grown on the slops bordering the River Thongue, which flows into the Hérault near St Thibéry.

I visited the Domaine de la Serre, near the village of St Thibéry, where M. Tobéna has 20 hectares of vines producing Côtes de Thongue. He makes a wine he describes as 'Rouge Tradition' from a blend of Carignan, Grenache and Cinsaut, as well as varietal Merlot, Cabernet Sauvignon and Syrah. Others

Opposite: The Château de Cassan near Pézenas in the *département* of Hérault.

include a rosé produced from Syrah and Grenache and a light red called 'Vin d'une Nuit,' from pure Grenache, which is labelled Vin de Pays d'Oc. M. Tobéna also makes a small quantity of white wine from a blend of Grenache Blanc, Muscat and Chasselas.

The Domaine de Bellevue, aptly named, is set on the crest of a hill a short distance to the west of the village of Montblanc, from where it overlooks the valley of the Thongue. Here Mme Hélène Péra farms 30 hectares of vines producing an excellent range of Vins de Pays.

The red wines include oak-aged Merlots and Cabernet Sauvignons, and another which is a blend of 60% Merlot and 40% Cabernet Sauvignon and left for one year in oak before bottling. A rosé is produced from Cinsaut and Cabernet Sauvignon, and white varietal wines are made from Sauvignon Blanc and Chardonnay, with the latter also offered as an oak-aged alternative.

Other notable independent producers of Côtes de Thongue include the Domaine de la Croix Belle at Puissalicon, the Château de Coussergues at Montblanc, the Prieuré d'Amilhac near Servian, the Domaine de la Condamine l'Evêque at Nézignan, the Domaine Deshenrys at Alignan du Vent, and the Domaine des Arbouries at Magalas.

Côtes de Thongues is also produced at a number of co-operatives, including Montblanc, Magalas and Puissalicon. At the last, a village with a fine old church, a feudal château, remains of ramparts and a fortified gateway, the co-operative makes an excellent, modestly-priced Merlot as well as red, white and rosé wines blended from the usual traditional varieties.

ARDAILHOU

Due south of the Côtes de Thongue, the Canal du Midi begins its journey from the mouth of the River Hérault, thus linking the Mediterranean to the Atlantic-bound River Garonne in the heart of the Midi. The village of Cers, lying on the north bank of the canal, is the centre of a small appellation called Vin de Pays de l'Ardailhou. It includes the villages of Villeneuve, Portiragnes, Sérignan, Sauvian, Valras, Vendres and Vias, and has a total vineyard area of 2,600 hectares. The co-operative at Cers produces a red wine using Merlot and Syrah, a white from Ugni Blanc and Terret Blanc, a Syrah rosé and a Chardonnay.

COTEAUX DU LIBRON

The Coteaux du Libron is a Vin de Pays appellation granted to the vineyards on the hills bordering the River Libron near Béziers. Production is based largely at the Cave Co-opérative at Boujan-sur-Libron. There is no *caveau* here, but the wines are on sale to the public at the Béziers co-operative on the eastern outskirts of the town. Here, a basic red is made from Cabernet Sauvignon and Merlot, a white from 100% Terret

Blanc, and a Syrah rosé. At the Domaine du Bosc at Lignan-sur-Orb an independent producer, M. Gilles Vidal, makes an excellent oak-aged Cabernet Sauvignon.

COTEAUX D'ENSÉRUNE

From Béziers the Canal du Midi leads westwards through a wine-growing region called the Coteaux d'Ensérune. It is named after an archaeological site known as Oppidum d'Ensérune, near the village of Poilhes, where numerous Roman remains have been discovered. Nearby is a curious drained lake, the Etang de Capestang.

The main feature of the region is the Canal du Midi, whose course can be traced clearly in the distance

Above: The Canal du Midi near Capestang in the *département* of Hérault.

by the winding alley of plane trees, over 4,500 of them, which shade its banks. The canal's existence is due to the obsessive entrepreneurial drive of one man, Paul Riquet.

Born in Béziers, Riquet is buried in Toulouse cathedral and is still regarded by the people of the Midi as a cross between legend and hero. He was a salt-tax collector and a wealthy man, but his pursuit of the project lost him both his fortune and his health. He died in 1680, when only a few miles of the canal remained to be built. It opened in 1681.

The undertaking involved digging a vast trench linking the rivers of the Garonne and Aude, and diverting water to fill the trench from the streams which flow from the Montagne Noir. It also involved building the longest stretch of level lock-free canal and the world's first canal tunnel 180 yards long. It was completed in six days – a rather effective reply to those who said it couldn't be done.

The Domaine de Guéry is a vineyard which borders the canal near the town of Capestang. Its *caveau*, just a stone's throw from the bank, is a popular stopping place for the numerous pleasure boats and barges which pass by each day during the summer. Here, M. Max Tastevy makes excellent Vin de Pays as well as his fine oak-aged AOC St Chinian.

The Tastevy family have been making wine in this region for a thousand years, and the present vineyard of 36 hectares has been established for over two hundred. In M. Tastevy's ancient *chais* are rows of vast oak casks over a hundred years old, holding 32,000 litres apiece – so huge that they had to be constructed inside the building. He makes a red Vin de Pays from Merlot and Carignan, and a rosé from a blend of Grenache and Cinsaut, with just a little Syrah. A blended white wine is made from Grenache Blanc and Carignan Blanc, as well as an excellent Chardonnay.

The Cave Co-opérative of neighbouring Nissan-lez-Ensérune also has a fine reputation for Vin de Pays. It is one of a group of six co-operatives vinifying the grapes from a total vineyard area of 6,000 hectares. A white wine is produced from a blend of Ugni Blanc, Clairette and Chardonnay; both red and rosé from Carignan, Syrah and Grenache; and varietal reds are made from Merlot and Cabernet Sauvignon. Both Chardonnay and Sauvignon Blanc are also produced here with the Vin de Pays d'Oc label.

If the idea of staying beside the Canal du Midi appeals to you, it would be difficult to find a hotel closer to it than the Auberge de l'Arbousier, in the village of Homps, near Olonzac. Comfortably furnished, with excellent food, the hotel is set in an ancient Knights Templars' commanderie a few paces from the canal side.

COTEAUX DE FONTCAUDE

About 10 kilometres to the north of Capestang is the ancient Abbaye de Fontcaude, hidden away in a small valley in the *garrigue*. Dating from the twelfth century, it was burned and badly damaged in 1577 during the Wars of Religion. It was bought by the association of the Friends of Fontcaude in 1969, since when it has been progressively restored. The abbey gives its name to the local Vin de Pays, Coteaux de Fontcaude, which includes the communes of Creissan, Quarante, Cazedarnes, Cébazan, Cruzy and Puisserguier.

A group of five Caves Co-opératives called Les 1,000 Vignerons, whose headquarters are at Cébezan, produce wines from a total vineyard area of 3,000 hectares, using the latest techniques and equipment to make both Vin de Pays and AOC St Chinian.

The Château de Rouire, built in the nineteenth century, houses a wine museum in its cellars and is open to visitors every day of the week, its *caveau* selling both Coteaux d'Ensérune and Fontcaude as well as AOC St Chinian. Varietal reds from Cabernet Sauvignon and Merlot are made here, as well as Syrah rosé, Chardonnay and Sauvignon Blanc. The *caveau* represents *vignerons* at Creissan, Maureilhan, Puisserguier and Quarante.

Château Milhau-Lacugue is a independent producer with 50 hectares of vines on the hills a few kilometres to the north of Puisserguier. The domaine was originally established by the Hospitallers of St John in the fifteenth century. Here, Mme Emilienne Lacugue produces both Coteaux de Fontcaude and AOC St Chinian, using about half the total vineyard area for each.

Perhaps the most interesting of the Vins de Pays made by the domaine is a Chenin Blanc which is both vinified and matured in oaks casks before bottling. A red wine made from 100% Carignan is also aged for up to six months in oak, and there is a Blanc de Blancs produced from a blend of Carignan Blanc, Terret Blanc, Clairette and Grenache Blanc.

Other notable independent producers of Coteaux

Vineyards of the Minervois near the village of Minerve in the *département* of Hérault.

de Fontcaude include the Domaine des Mathurins at Cazedarnes and the domaines of Lussau, Mairan and Mallemont at Puisserguier.

CÔTES DU BRIAN

The Minervois is a region of mountainous *garrigue* between Béziers and Carcassonne at the foot of the Montagne Noir. It is one of the oldest of all the Mediterranean vineyards and was chosen by the Romans to be the location of the first vines planted in Languedoc-Roussillon. The region is named after the fortified village of Minerve, built on a rocky outcrop in the winding canyon of the river Cesse.

This remote and atmospheric village was the site of one of the cruellest reprisals carried out by Simon de Montfort in his crusade against the Cathars. Almost surrounded by gorges and cliffs, it was one of the last remaining pockets of resistance, and de Montfort arrived with an army of 7,000 men, determined to take it. The siege had lasted for 7 weeks when, deprived of water, the remaining 180 villagers surrendered and were offered the choice of conversion to Catholicism or death. They were all burned to death in a huge fire at the foot of the castle.

The AOC wines of the Minervois are renowned, but the region also has a less well-known Vin de Pays appellation, Côtes du Brian, which covers 13 communes, of which Olonzac is the centre.

The co-operative at Olonzac produces a red Côtes du Brian from 100% Merlot, a rosé from pure Syrah, and a white blended from Grenache Blanc, Maccabeo and Marsanne. A superior red, 'Cuvée St Martin d'Onairac', is made from Merlot and Cabernet Sauvignon and is matured in oak casks before bottling. The co-operatives of Azillanet and Montouliers also produce Côtes du Brian.

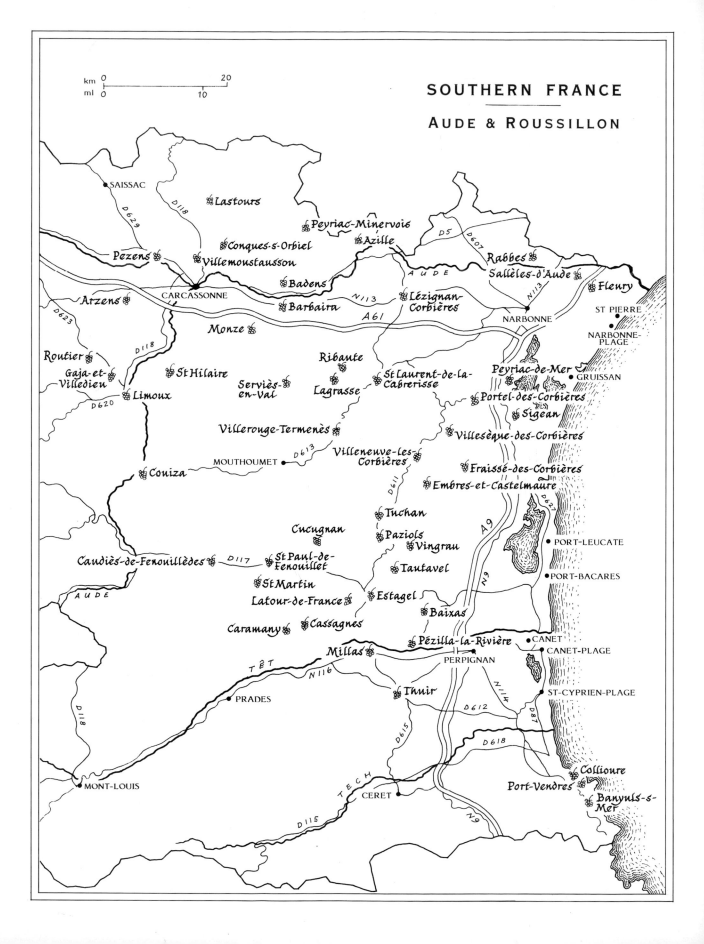

km 0 ——————————— 20
ml 0 ——————————— 10

SOUTHERN FRANCE

AUDE & ROUSSILLON

SAISSAC

🍇 Lastours

🍇 Peyriac-Minervois

🍇 Conques-s-Orbiel   🍇 Azille

Pezens 🍇   🍇 Villemoustausson

🍇 Badens   Rabbes
🍇 Sallèles-d'Aude 🍇   🍇 Fleury

Arzens 🍇   CARCASSONNE   🍇 Lézignan-
🍇 Barbaira   Corbières

🍇 Monze   NARBONNE   ST PIERRE

NARBONNE-
PLAGE

Routier 🍇   Ribaute   🍇 Peyriac-de-Mer   GRUISSAN
Gaja-et-🍇   🍇 St Hilaire   🍇 St Laurent-de-la-
Villedieu   Serviès-🍇   🍇 Cabrerisse   🍇 Portel-des-Corbières
en-Val   Lagrasse   🍇 Sigean

🍇 Limoux   🍇 Villesèque-des-Corbières

Villerouge-Termenès 🍇

MOUTHOUMET   Villeneuve-les-🍇   🍇 Fraissé-des-Corbières
🍇 Couiza   Corbières   🍇 Embres-et-Castelmaure

🍇 Tuchan

Cucugnan 🍇   🍇 Paziols
🍇 Vingrau   PORT-LEUCATE

Caudiès-de-Fenouillèdes 🍇   🍇 St Paul-de-   🍇 Tautavel   PORT-BACARES
Fenouillet
🍇 St Martin   🍇 Estagel
Latour-de-France 🍇   🍇 Baixas   ST-CYPRIEN-PLAGE

Caramany 🍇   🍇 Cassagnes
🍇 Pézilla-la-Rivière   CANET
Millas 🍇   CANET-PLAGE

PERPIGNAN

PRADES   🍇 Thuir

MONT-LOUIS   CERET   🍇 Collioure
Port-Vendres 🍇   🍇 Banyuls-s-
Mer

AUDE

The Étang de Bages in the *département* of Aude.

In the case of the Aude it is surprising that the French authorities did not choose to make one of their few exceptions to the rule of naming a *département* after its principal river, and name it after the mountain range which practically fills it, the Corbières.

The *département* of the Aude is bordered in the east by the Mediterranean, with only a relatively narrow coastal strip between the sea and the foothills of the Corbières. A steep ridge between the mountain range and the valley of the River Maury creates the southern border. In the east and north the limits of the *département* are marked by the curving course of the River Aude as it flows from its source in the Pyrenees, to its estuary between Narbonne and Béziers.

The landscape of the Corbières is one of surprising variety, ranging from bare, rocky escarpments to extensive areas of dense *garrigue*, softly rounded hills terraced with vines, wide pastoral valleys and narrow defiles with white-water rivers running through them.

The countryside is known as the Pays Cathares on account of its history and the many surviving castles which were built to defend the Cathars against the rigorous persecution of the Albigensian crusades. The imposing remains of castles like Peyrepertuse, Quéribus, Aguilar, Durfort and Villerouge seem to loom up on every craggy height.

The land here is planted less extensively with vines than in the Hérault but it is, nonetheless, a region of France where viticulture dominates the way of life and the economy of the region. Coteaux du Languedoc and Corbières are the main AOC appellations, along with other smaller regions like Fitou and Rivesaltes, but the *département* is also divided into smaller local territories which give their names to the wide range of Vins de Pays and VDQS wines which are also produced.

CUCUGNAN

The most southerly Vin de Pays appellation is that of Cucugnan, an ancient village strikingly situated on a rocky knoll in the valley of the River Verdouble, under the shadow of the ruins of the thirteenth-century Château de Peyrepertuse. The Cave Co-opérative of the village is the sole producer of the wine from the vineyards in the surrounding countryside. Only red

The wine village of Cucugnan in the *département* of Aude.

wine is made here, from a blend of Carignan, Grenache and Syrah.

TORGAN

To the east of Cucugnan the Verdouble enters the valley of the River Torgan near the village of Padern, where the outline of another ruined castle dominates the skyline. Between Padern and Tuchan the road provides sweeping views over a wide, shallow valley which is filled with vineyards as far as the eye can see.

Vin de Pays du Torgan is produced by the Cave Coopérative in the village of Tuchan, at the foot of the 900-metre peak of the Montagne de Tauch. The *cave* produces a red from 100% Carignan and a rosé from Cinsaut, which is supplied only *en vrac*.

The neighbouring village of Paziols has a very progressive co-operative which has been selling direct to the public since 1946. Situated at the extreme southeastern corner of the Aude, the co-operative has vineyards which fall within the Fitou and Rivesaltes appellations as well as the valley of the Torgan and Corbières.

Grapes are supplied to the co-operative by 260 producers from a total of 720 hectares of vines. Previously known as the Vins de Pays de Coteaux Cathares, the area of production is spread between the villages of Davejean, Dernacueillette, Duilhac, Massac, Montgaillard, Padern, Rouffiac-des-Corbières and Tuchan.

Carignan represents the principal grape variety used in both red and rosé Vins de Pays de Torgan, but a smaller percentage of Cinsaut, Grenache, Syrah, Mourvedre, Terret and the Cabernets are also used. One superior wine is produced which is aged for eight months in oak and sold with the label of 'Baron de la Tour'.

VALLÉE DU PARADIS

To the north-east of Tuchan, the D 611 passes the hilltop castle of Aguilar on its way through a valley bordered by *garrigue*-covered hillsides to the village of Villeneuve-les-Corbières. This is the centre of production for Vin de Pays de la Vallée du Paradis.

Above: The River Torgan near the wine village of Paziols in the *département* of Aude. Overleaf: Vineyards near the wine village of Padern in the valley of the River Verdouble.

At the Villeneuve co-operative a red wine is made from Carignan and Grenache with a small proportion of Syrah, and at the time of writing – 1993 – they had produced their first harvest for a white Vin de Pays made exclusively from Grenache Blanc.

Although widely produced in the region, many of the larger co-operatives supply Vin de Pays only *en vrac*, and the emphasis is strongly on red wine production. Exceptions to this are the co-operatives at Fraissé-des-Corbières, where there is a restored thirteenth-century château, and at Villesèque-des-Corbières, a few kilometres to the north. An enjoyable scenic drive can be made by following the quiet country road through the mountains to the villages of Embres-et-Castelmaure, St Jean-de-Barrou and Fraissé-des-Corbières.

Coteaux du Littoral Audois

From here the D 205 descends from the Col de Souil to Roquefort-des-Corbières on the coastal plain. Here, and around the edges of the Etang de Bages and the villages of Sigean, Portel-des-Corbières, Leucate and Peyriac-de-Mer, is the production area for Vins de Pays des Coteaux du Littoral Audois. This wine is predominantly red and produced largely from the Carignan variety by a group of three Caves Co-opératives. The one based in Peyriac has an excellent *caveau*.

A short distance to the south of Narbonne, on the N 9, the D 105 leads through the vineyards planted around the edge of the lagoon to the villages of Bages and Peyriac-sur-Mer, offering a succession of captivating views. The little village of Bages is built on a rock overlooking the lake with a web of steep narrow streets rising up from a small quay where fishing boats are pulled up on to the beach with their nets draped over rickety wooden causeways to dry.

The lake shore is a bird-watcher's paradise where all manner of water birds congregate along the water's edge. Large flocks of flamingos are a common sight. The small town of Peyriac is a delightful spot with a quiet lakeside waterfront and a number of beaches

The Cathar castle of Aguilar near the village of Tuchan in the *département* of Aude.

which can be reached along a rough road. Although popular in the daytime during the summer months, the town has little hotel accommodation and has retained an unspoilt, quiet charm.

COTEAUX DU TERMENÈS

To the west of Villeneuve, a road leads over the mountains through an attractive pocket of countryside to Quintillan and Palairac before descending into the gorges of the River Torgan and the village of Davejean, which has a twelfth-century church and fountain.

North of Davejean, amid spectacular scenery, are the remains of the castles of Termes and Durfort and the very attractive medieval village of Villerouge-Termenès, with its fine twelfth-century château.

A medieval festival is held here in the summer to mark the death of the last of the Cathar zealots, Guilhem Bélibaste. He was burned at the stake in 1321 and his death signalled the end of the Cathar church.

The celebrations held between July and September include a costume spectacular held on Wednesdays and Sundays, a medieval banquet on Saturdays, and an exhibition which traces Guilhem's last days.

The village has a Cave Co-opérative which produces the region's Vin de Pays. Coteaux du Termenès. Out of season the *cave* only opens once a fortnight, but a builder working nearby took me to one of the *vignerons* who lives in a cottage next door. He produced a few bottles from his garage for me to try, including a red made from 100% Carignan and a white from Grenache Blanc, unsophisticated but enjoyable country wines.

COTEAUX DE LA CABRERISSE

To the north of Villerouge, the landscape flattens out and becomes more open, with huge expanses of vineyards stretching away towards the horizon. The small town of St Laurent-de-la-Cabrerisse is the production centre for the local Vin de Pays, Coteaux de la

The wine village of Portel-des-Corbières in the *département* of Aude.

Cabrerisse, along with the villages of Montséret and Thézan-des-Corbières.

At Thézan a rosé is produced from a blend of Grenache Gris, Syrah and Cinsaut, while at St Laurent a red is made from 100% Carignan. At the latter, a *primeur* is released on 15 October each year which is made exclusively from Syrah using 30% carbonic maceration.

Nearby, at Château Caraguilhes, Vin de Pays des Coteaux de la Cabrerisse is also produced by an independent wine-maker with the label, 'Domaine de la Bouletière.' Here, Michèle and Lionel Favre use biological production methods to make red wines from 50% Merlot with 25% each of Carignan and Alicante, as well as a rosé produced from 50/50 Cinsaut and Carignan.

A white from Bourboulenc and Carignan Blanc is also produced from time to time, but in limited quantities and not every year. Of the total of 128 hectares approximately one-fifth is used to produce Vin de Pays. Château Caraguilhes dates from the sixteenth century, when it was a dependency of the Cistercian abbey of Fontfroide, a short drive to the east and surrounded by ravines. Close by is the thirteenth-century Château de Gaussan.

CÔTES DE LÉZIGNAN

To the north of St Laurent-de-la-Cabrerisse is the busy little market town of Lézignan-Corbières, the region's capital. Above the rooftops rises the imposing bell tower of a church which was reconstructed in the twelfth century on the site of an earlier Roman church. There is a large and varied collection of old wine-making equipment on display in the museum of wine at the Caves Saury-Serrès.

The town's Cave Co-opérative, built in 1909 in a distinctly *Belle Epoque* architectural style, contains an array of massive oak casks. It was the first co-operative to be established in the *département* of the Aude.

Red, white and rosé Vins de Pays de Côtes de Lézignan are produced here from the vineyards which surround the town. The red wine is produced from a blend of 80% Merlot and 20% Carignan, the rosé is 100% Cinsaut, and the white is made from pure Carignan Blanc. A *primeur*, on sale from 15 October, is made from Syrah using 100% carbonic maceration.

Nearby, the co-operative at Conilhac-Corbières produces an interesting trio of Côtes de Lézignan: a red from 50/50 Carignan and Cabernet Sauvignon, a rosé from 80% Cinsaut and 20% Grenache Gris, and a white from 100% Chasan. The last is a newly developed grape variety which is being quite widely planted in the Languedoc. It is a cross between Chardonnay and Listan, which is also known as Palomino in Spain's Jerez region.

HAUTERIVE EN PAYS D'AUDE
The Vin de Pays d'Hauterive en Pays d'Aude is produced in the countryside to the south of Lézignan, and the appellation is restricted to the villages of Fontcouverte, Ornaisons, Talairan, Tournissan, Tourouzelle, Fabrezan, Montséret and Ferrals-les-Corbières.

The name originates from the Domaine de Hauterive, which was a dependency of the abbey of Fontfroide during the Middle Ages. Although there is an annual production of around 25,000 hectolitres, it proved difficult to find in bottles, for it is sold largely *en vrac* by the co-operatives. However, I was told that there are plans to market more of the wine in bottles within the next year or so.

A current exception is a *primeur* produced by the co-operative at Ferrals, which is released on 15 October with the label 'Fleur d'Automne'. Made using carbonic maceration from a blend of Syrah and Grenache, it is very popular locally and widely promoted in restaurants.

I did not have to opportunity to visit, but the Domaine de Hauterive le Vieux near the village of Ornaisons is an independent producer of the appellation with a high reputation locally.

A very pleasant place to stay in the region can be found in the village of Fabrezan at the Hôtel le Clos des Souquets, which has just five stylishly decorated rooms beside a small swimming pool and a charming restaurant and terrace overlooking another pool. The

food is excellent, and there are five associated *gîtes* nearby in a house in the village.

VAL DE CESSE
The Vin de Pays appellation Val de Cesse is produced from the vineyards around the villages of Ginestas, Pouzols-Minervois, Ventenac-en-Minervois, St Marcel, Salleles-d'Aude, Ouveillan, Bize-Minervois and Mailhac. This rather flat and open landscape to the north-west of Narbonne is threaded by the meandering rivers of the Aude and Cesse as well as the Canal du Midi.

The majority of this Vin de Pays is produced by Caves Co-opératives. The *caveau* at Ventenac-en-Minervois is set in a lovely old château on the banks of the Canal du Midi which was converted for its present use in 1938. Here, a red wine is produced from a blend of Merlot, Carignan and Syrah, a rosé from 70% Cabernet Sauvignon and 30% Syrah, and a white wine from Maccabeo and Ugni Blanc. At the co-operative of nearby Pouzols-Minervois, a very good, modestly priced *vin de cépage* is made from Merlot.

The Domaine de Truilhas, a few kilometres to the north-west of Salleles-d'Aude on the banks of the Canal du Midi, is one of the few independent producers of Val de Cesse, making only Vin de Pays from 45 hectares of vines. Here the Comte de Saint-Exupéry produces an interesting selection of wines which are mainly sold direct to the public and local restaurants. Red varietal wines are made from both Merlot and Cabernet Sauvignon, with the latter also used to make a rosé. In addition they make a pure Chardonnay, and this variety is also vinified as a sparkling wine using the *méthode champenoise*.

COTEAUX DE NARBONNE
The vineyards in the vicinity of Narbonne are entitled to the Vin de Pays appellation Coteaux de Narbonne, but it is one which is gradually disappearing in favour of Vin de Pays de l'Aude or d'Oc. I was only able to find one example of a co-operative wine at the Moussan *cave*, where an inexpensive rosé is produced from Carignan and Cinsaut together with a red wine using Carignan and Grenache.

M. Hérail, at the Château de Rabbes, to the north of Cuxac-d'Aude, is the president of the Coteaux de Narbonne association and an independent producer of the appellation. Unfortunately he was away when I visited, but Mme Hérail told me the domaine produced a range of varietal wines from Chardonnay, Merlot, Cabernet Sauvignon and Grenache, the latter also used to make a rosé.

CÔTES DE PÉRIGNAN

Between Narbonne and the sea is a curious rugged landscape called the Montagne de la Clape. Here, outcrops of silvery limestone rock covered with dense green pines rise up in stark contrast to the rather dull, featureless coastline of Narbonne-Plage. At the southern edge of the Montagne is the attractive old fortified fishing port of Gruissan, built on a circular grid pattern.

The region has its own Vin de Pays appellation, Côtes de Pérignan, which is made both by Cave Co-opératives and independent producers. The co-operative at Fleury produces a red Merlot, a white wine from Grenache Blanc and Maccabeo, and a rosé from Grenache and Cinsaut.

One of the most notable of the independent producers is the Château de Pech Celeyran, a kilometre or so to the east of Coursan, where an extremely interesting range of Vins de Pays are made in addition to AOC La Clape. The domaine has a total vineyard area of 90 hectares, about half of which is used to produce Vins de Pays.

These include varietal white wines from Chardonnay, Maccabeo and Viognier, together with red wines using Pinot Noir and Cabernet Sauvignon, as well as a blended red and a rosé sold *en vrac*. A particularly notable wine is made from Chardonnay which is both vinified and aged in oak *foudres* before bottling.

The nearby Domaine de Roquelastours is another highly-regarded producer of Vin de Pays with an excellent oak-aged red wine made from a blend of Merlot, Cabernet Sauvignon and Grenache, together with a Syrah rosé and a varietal Merlot.

VAL D'ORBIEU

To the west of Narbonne the little River Orbieu runs a parallel course to the Aude. The Vin de Pays du Val d'Orbieu is produced mainly from a cluster of villages between Lézignan and Narbonne and is marketed directly by a single producer, largely to supermarkets, restaurants and specialist shops in the region, as Vin de Pays d'Oc, or d'Aude. The co-operative, Le Pavillon des Vins, is just outside Narbonne on the Route de Moussan.

Some of the vineyards belonging to this appellation, about 20 hectares in all, are situated further to the west around the village of Ribaute, near Lagrasse. There is a co-operative here, opposite which, in the garage of a small bungalow, is a make-shift *caveau* where the wines can be tasted and bought.

Red only is produced here from a blend of 80% Carignan and 10% each of Grenache and Cinsaut. Biologically approved production methods are used to make these wines – not, I was told, for reasons of environmental concern but because the market for these wines, largely in Germany, demands it.

VAL DE DAGNE

Further to the west along the valley of the Orbieu is the medieval walled village of Lagrasse, which was the capital of the Corbières until the middle of the nineteenth century. It has a network of narrow cobbled streets, with many fifteenth-century houses as well as the fine fourteenth-century church of St Michel.

An ancient stone hump-backed bridge gives access to an abbey which was founded in the tenth century under Charlemagne. It is now occupied, and is being restored by a Byzantine Catholic religious order, but it can be visited. The village is known for its pottery market held during August and, more recently established, a leather market during July.

From Lagrasse the D 3 leads westwards through the gorges of the Alsou to a beautiful open valley patterned by vines and bordered by mountain slopes. It is here, from the vineyards around the villages of Lagrasse, Serviès-en-Val, Montlaur and Monze, that the Vin de Pays du Val de Dagne is produced.

At the village of Serviès-en-Val there is a seventeenth-century château with a lovely ochre façade flanked by towers and complemented by a terraced garden. The village has a small *caveau* in a cottage opposite the Cave Co-opérative named after Joseph Delteil, a well-known contemporary French writer from the region. A red wine is produced here from Carignan and Merlot, using carbonic maceration, and since 1992 a Chardonnay has been produced from a newly-planted vineyard of just 2 hectares.

Nearby, the village of Villars-en-Val has an imposing château and a pretty eleventh-century church surrounded by cypress and olive trees. It is

built on a terrace, from which there are sweeping views over the valley. The co-operative at the neighbouring village of Montlaur produces a red Val de Dagne from 100% Merlot, and has recently planted a parcel of Chardonnay and Chasan vines which will come into production in 1997.

CITÉ DE CARCASSONNE

The city of Carcassonne, only a short distance from here, is perhaps the most perfectly preserved medieval fortified town in Europe, with a most unusual double circle of walls and elaborate entrance gates. Its present state is largely due to the enormous efforts of the architect Eugène Viollet-le-Duc, who restored the city in the mid-nineteenth century. The oldest parts date from Visigothic and Roman times.

A walk around the ramparts gives one the impression that the city must have been virtually impregnable, but it suffered badly at the hands of the notorious Simon de Montfort during the Albigensian crusades. Any medieval ambience inside the old city is rather diminished by the presence of numerous souvenir shops selling suits of plastic armour and broad swords. Seen in the distance, on the other hand, from the vineyards which surround it, the city makes a much more atmospheric impression.

The Vin de Pays de la Cité de Carcassonne is produced from the vineyards around a dozen or so villages which encircle the city: Trèbes, Villedubert, Pennautier, Montirat, Berriac, Palaja, Cazilhac, Cavanac, Couffoulens, Preixan and Rouffiac-d'Aude.

The wines are produced by many of the local Caves Co-opératives and vary considerably in terms of both grape varieties and character. At Trèbes, for instance, where the *caveau* occupies a few shelves in the garden centre opposite the winery, they make an oak-aged Cabernet Sauvignon and a rosé from 100% Cinsaut. A red *primeur* is also produced from Merlot, Cinsaut and Syrah, and a normal blended red from Merlot and Carignan.

The co-operative at Pezens on the N 113, a few kilometres west of Carcassone, is supplied by *vignerons* with plots around the village of Pennautier. A red Cité de Carcassonne is made here from a blend of 60% Merlot and a balance of Grenache, and they also

Opposite: Vineyards near the village of Ribaute in the *département* of Aude.

The medieval village of Lagrasse in the northern foothills of the Corbières.

produce Vins de Pays Côtes de Lastours and VDQS Cabardès.

I did not have the chance to visit the vineyard, but the Domaine Ste Marie des Pins near the village of Verzeille is an independent producer with a sound local reputation for white *vins de cépage* made from Chardonnay and Sauvignon.

CABARDÈS

Cabardès or, to give it its full name, Cabardès-Orbiel, is a VDQS appellation granted in 1973 to a designated area of vineyards to the north of Carcassone and west of the Minervois, in the hills bordering the valley of the River Orbiel.

It covers about 40 communes and comprises a total of 2,200 hectares producing primarily red wine made from traditional Mediterranean grape varieties, although some south-western varieties are permitted. A small amount of rosé is also produced. The Cabardès

made by the co-operative at Pezens, for example, is made from 50% Merlot, 35% Grenache and 15% Cabernet Sauvignon.

Among the independent producers of the appellation are the Domaine des Caunettes Hautes near Moussoulens, Château Rivals near Villemoustaussou, Château Salatis near Conques-sur-Orbiel, Château la Bastide and the Domaine Loupia at Pennautier.

CÔTES DE LASTOURS

The Vin de Pays de Côtes de Lastours is an appellation granted to vineyards around the medieval village of Lastours, which lies 15 kilometres or so to the north of Carcassonne.

The co-operative at Pezens produces a red Côtes de Lastours from 80% Cabernet Sauvignon and 20% Merlot, a rosé from 60% Grenache Gris, 30% Cinsaut and 10% Cabernet Sauvignon, and a Blanc de Blancs from 100% Ugni Blanc.

I visited Wenny and Gabriel Fari at the Château de Brau, near the village of Villemoustaussou, where they make both Cabardès and Côtes de Lastours wines from 25 hectares of vines which they farm using biological techniques. They told me the period of transition from normal agricultural methods took three years to accomplish and they made the change as much for the sake of their very young family as for any wider environmental considerations. Their vines include Merlot, Cabernet Sauvignon, Grenache, Fer Servadou, Carignan, Cinsaut, Syrah and Cot.

From a blend of Mediterranean varieties they make a traditional Cabardès called 'Cuvée Bleue', and one which includes a proportion of Merlot and Cabernet Sauvignon, called 'Cuvée Première', as well as 'Cuvée Exquise', which is matured for one year in oak casks and capable of keeping for five years or more. The Côtes de Lastours made here is a 50/50 blend of Merlot and Grenache.

Their Vin de Pays wines include a Blanc de Blancs produced from a blend of 60% Chardonnay and Roussanne, as well as a pure Chardonnay, both of which are labelled Vin de Pays de l'Aude. Although they would be permitted to use the Côtes de Lastours appellation for these wines, they feel this name is more strongly associated with red wines.

The village of Lastours is impressively sited beneath a monumental rock upon which are set the remains of four towers known as Caberet, Régine, Surdespine and Quéritinheux. They were built to protect the passage of valuable minerals mined in the neighbouring Montagne Noire to the Mediterranean ports. Nearby is the charming small fortified village of Conques-sur-Orbiel, the stalactite caverns of Limousis and the gorges of Clamoux.

COTEAUX DE PEYRIAC

About 20 kilometres south-east of Lastours is the Minervois town of Peyriac, which gives its name to the region's Vins de Pays, Coteaux de Peyriac. This is produced from 17 villages, of which two are in the *département* of Hérault. The major part of the production is by the co-operatives and a large proportion of this is sold in bulk to supermarkets.

The co-operative at Laure-Minervois produces red, rosé and white Coteaux de Peyriac, which is sold in 32-litre 'cubitainers', a non-rigid plastic container held inside a cardboard box. However, they sell a Merlot in bottles, as well as a red made from a blend of Carignan, Merlot and Cinsaut. A white wine in bottles is also produced, from 100% Chasan, with the label Vin de Pays de l'Aude.

A few kilometres to the south-west of Laure-Minervois on the D 135 is the Château Gibalux, an ancient priory of the convent of Caunes-Minervois, with a history dating back to the beginning of the twelfth century. Here Marie-Jean and Jean-Baptiste Bonnet produce AOC Minervois from a total of 50 hectares of vines and Coteaux de Peyriac from 30 hectares. A varietal red Vin de Pays is made here from Merlot, as well as an oak-aged Chardonnay and one which is bottled directly from the vat.

HAUTS DE BADENS

A short distance to the south of Laure-Minervois is the little hill village of Badens, overlooking the valley of the Aude. The Vin de Pays des Hauts de Badens is one of the smallest appellations in the Aude, with just two independent producers.

One of them, Pierre Cros, is to be found in the village itself. He farms 12 hectares of vines planted on the slopes below it, from which he produces both red and rosé wines. The reds are a blend of Carignan, Syrah and Grenache, while the rosé is made by replacing the Carignan with Cinsaut. He also produces a *primeur* from Syrah alone, using normal fermentation techniques.

A kilometre or so outside the village is the Château de la Grave, where for many generations the Orosquette family have produced both AOC Minervois and Vins de Pays. There are 43 hectares in current production, from which M. Orosquette makes red, white and rosé Vins de Pays. The traditional red is a mixture of 80% Carignan and Merlot, but a red is also made from a 50/50 blend of Merlot and Cabernet Sauvignon. There is a rosé from Cinsaut and Grenache Gris, and a white from Chasan, Chardonnay and Sauvignon Blanc. M. Orosquette also produces *primeurs* in all three colours which are available from 15 October.

COTEAUX DE MIRAMONT

From the village of Badens you can see the Montagne d'Alaric rising steeply on the other side of the Aude valley. At the highest point of over 500 metres are the ruins of the Château de Miramont, reached from a road heading up from the town of Barbaira.

On the outskirts of the town is Château Hélène, where Mme Marie-Hélène produces both AOC Corbières and Vin de Pays des Coteaux de Miramont from 25 hectares of vineyards planted on the Alaric slopes.

'Vin d'une Nuit' is a name often given to a pale rosé, but here it is a light red wine, made from a blend of 80% Cinsaut and 20% Syrah, which is left to macerate for 15 hours before the juice is racked from the lees. A rosé is also produced from a very short period of maceration using a mixture of 80% Cinsaut and 20% Carignan. In addition, a more traditional red is produced using 60% Carignan, 30% Syrah and 10% Cinsaut.

CÔTES DE LA MALAPÈRE

Twenty kilometres or so to the south-west of Carcassonne is a region known as the Pays de Razès, a countryside of open undulating hills, with meadows, woods, fields of grain and vineyards. This, and the surrounding region, are the production area for the Côtes de la Malapère, a VDQS appellation established in 1976. It was the result of a bold experiment, initiated in the 1960s, to establish new grape varieties which could benefit from a climate influenced both by the Mediterranean and by the more moderate conditions of south-west France.

One of the main producers of this appellation is the Caves de Razès, a co-operative situated on the D 623 near the village of Routier, 12 kilometres or so to the north-west of Limoux. The wines here are based principally on a mixture of Mediterranean and south-western varieties such as Merlot, Cot and Cinsaut, as well as a variable proportion of Syrah, Cabernet Sauvignon, Cabernet Franc and Grenache.

The little village of Routier has an attractive fifteenth-century château from which Michèle Lezerat produces Côtes de la Malapère from around 50 hectares of vines grown on the slopes around the village.

A few kilometres to the east of Routier is the tiny village of Malvies, where a château was built at the end of the eighteenth century on the site of a Gallo-Roman settlement. Here, from around 50 hectares of Merlot, Cabernet Franc and Cabernet Sauvignon, Mme Gourdou produces a fine oak-aged Côtes de la Malapère with the label 'Cuvée Château Guilhem'.

In the village of Arzens, some 12 kilometres or so to the north of Routier, and situated between the Cabardès and Côtes de la Malapère, the Cellier Jean de Gres produces wines with both appellations, as well as Vin de Pays de la Cité de Carcassonne – an indication of just how close together some of the Languedoc appellations can be.

CÔTES DE PROUILLE

In the north of the Razès region is the monastery of Prouille, which was founded in the thirteenth century. It lies a short distance to the west of the hill village of Montréal, where there is a Cave-Coopérative producing Côtes de la Malapère. The abbey has given its name to the local Vin de Pays, Côtes de Prouille, and the Caves de Razès make a particularly good Chardonnay with this label.

Twenty kilometres or so to the south-west is the delightful small town of Mirepoix. The town was established around a castle taken by Simon de Montfort and given to one of his knights, but it was destroyed by a catastrophic flood in 1279 and rebuilt in the form of the present *bastide* on the opposite side of the river. It has an unusually large central square, surrounded by houses supported on slender wooden arcades, which is reminiscent of many Spanish villages. One of the original fortified gateways still exists, and the cathedral, built between the thirteenth and fifteenth centuries, boasts the largest Gothic nave in France and a bell tower over 60 metres high.

Thirteen kilometres to the south-east is Camon, a village built around a Benedictine abbey which was founded in 923. Destroyed twice, in 1279 and 1494, the village was reconstructed and fortified at the beginning of the sixteenth century.

HAUTE-VALLÉE DE L'AUDE

A short distance to the south-east of the Razès is the town of Limoux, which lies in the upper Aude valley. The town is famed for its Blanquette, a sparkling white AOC wine made from the Mauzec variety with additions of Chardonnay and Chenin Blanc.

It claims to be the oldest sparkling wine in the world, with Champagne just a young upstart by comparison. The wine owes its existence to the monks of the abbey of neighbouring Ste Hilaire. The curious name of Blanquette, meaning white in the language of Oc, is attributed to the veil of fine white hairs which cover the undersides of the Mauzac vine leaves.

In regions where the Appellation d'Origine Contrôlée decrees a single colour or type of wine, there is

The vineyards of the valley of the River Orbieu and, beyond, the Montagne d'Alaric in the *département* of Aude.

often a Vin de Pays which fulfils the need for greater variety. Here the Vin de Pays de la Haute-Vallée de l'Aude, widely produced in the region, provides an interesting range of alternative wines. The largest producer of both Blanquette and Vin de Pays is the Cave Co-opérative at Limoux, which was founded in 1947 and now has around 700 members.

The co-operative produces a basic Haute-Vallée de l'Aude in red and rosé from a blend of Merlot and Cabernet, together with a superior red, blended from Merlot, Syrah, Cabernet Franc and Cabernet Sauvignon, which is aged in oak for up to a year.

The *cave* also produces, from one small group of growers, a varietal Chardonnay and a Moelleux Vendanges Tardives from Chenin Blanc. The latter is an intensely fruity, sweet white wine made from grapes which are left on the vine, often until late November, until they have partially dried, concentrating the juice.

M. Tribillac, in the neighbouring village of Gaja-et-Villedieu, is typical of many of the independent producers in the region, making mainly a traditional Blanquette but also using 10 hectares of Merlot and Cabernet Sauvignon to produce a red Vin de Pays. Near the southern limit of the wine region of the Aude valley, the Domaine de Mayrac, near Couiza, produces both varietal Cabernet Sauvignons and Chardonnays.

The vineyards extend over a wide area, from St Hilaire and Gardie, in the hills north-east of Limoux, south along the valley of the Aude to Quillan, close to the foothills of the Pyrenees. The fortified Benedictine monastery of St Hilaire is well worth visiting. It was founded in the eighth century, but the present building dates from twelfth century and also has a fine fifteenth-century Gothic cloister. The hilly landscape at the western edge of the Corbières, around the villages of Pieusse, St Hilaire and Gardie, is particularly attractive and supports some of the most favoured vineyards.

ROUSSILLON

Opposite: The wine village of Caramany in the *département* of Pyrénées-Orientales. Above: The hill village of Castelnou near Thuir in the *département* of Pyrénées-Orientales.

The most southerly *département* of France, the Pyrénées-Orientales, seems almost isolated from the rest of the country. Held in a mountainous triangle between the Corbières to the north, the Pyrenees to the west and the Alberes to the south, it only has the Mediterranean to provide a sense of space and release from the narrow mountain-locked valleys which make up the major part of the habitable interior.

Representing the smallest part of the region known as Languedoc Roussillon, it is, like the Pays Basque, a country which has a fiercely partisan character with a language and culture similar to Spain's Catalonia, a short distance to the south. Place names are written in both French and Catalan, bull fights are held throughout the region, and the Sardane is danced here to a reedy lilting music, as it is in the towns and villages of north-east Spain, where it is called the Sardana.

The region is richly endowed in many ways. Above all, the climate is welcoming, with an average of 325 days of sunshine a year, and the scenery is breathtaking, with snow-capped mountains, white-water rivers, rocky gorges, green valleys, dramatically perched villages and a gloriously scenic coastline.

The vineyards have two regional Appellations d'Origine Contrôlée. Côtes du Roussillon covers the wide area from the coastal plain between the Etang de Salses and the mouth of the Tech to the valleys of the Agly, Tet and Tech. The vineyards in the mountains to the south of the mouth of the River Tech have a separate appellation, Collioure. Vins Doux are a speciality here, and there are a number of separate appellations for these sweet fortified wines, Banyuls, Maury, Rivesaltes and Muscat de Rivesaltes.

There are six Vin de Pays appellations: Pyrénées-Orientales, which covers the whole *département*; Catalan, which includes the region to the south of Perpignan; Vals d'Agly, which covers the upper valley of the Agly around the villages of St Paul-de-Fenouillet and Latour de France; Côtes Catalanes, which is granted to the villages in the lower valley of the Agly and the coastal plain to the north of Perpignan; and Coteaux de Fenouillèdes, which encompasses the vineyards in the mountains to the south-west of St Paul-de-Fenouillèdes. Côte Vermeille is an appellation which covers the area defined by the

AOC of Collioure, and applies primarily to red wine which is sold largely in bulk by co-operatives to *négociants* and local supermarkets.

CATALAN

Vin de Pays Catalan is the largest and most important of the zonal appellations, with an annual production of 110,000 hectolitres. Much of the Vin de Pays production is handled by the numerous Caves Co-opératives, of which there is one in almost every community. Traditionally, the trend has been towards red wines made from Grenache Noir, Mourvèdre, Syrah and Carignan, but in recent years there has been extensive planting of Cabernet Sauvignon and Merlot. White wines are made from Grenache Blanc, Maccabeo, Muscat and Chardonnay.

The vineyards are situated around the small town of Thuir, in the centre of the region known as the Aspres, and extend to the villages of Castelnou, Camélas and Llupia. I visited the co-operative at Thuir, one of the larger and more progressive *caves* in the region. It was founded in 1924 with just a small group of producers, but has expanded considerably and today has a vat capacity of 80,000 hectolitres. It produces a white wine from 100% Maccabeo and a red from a blend of Grenache, Carignan and Merlot as well as a *primeur* which is on sale in the middle of October.

Among the independent producers of Vin de Pays Catalan is Domaine Laporte in the village of Château Roussillon, a few kilometres east of Perpignan. An interesting Blanc de Blancs is made here from the Muscat variety.

An attractive small market town, Thuir has a wine museum in the Celliers des Aspres, but the one place which should not be missed in the area is the hilltop village of Castelnou, which lies 6 kilometres or so to the west along the D 48.

Surrounded by vine-terraced mountainsides, the village is dominated by the Massif du Canigou rising up behind like a dark cloud. Inside a fortified gateway lies a maze of narrow cobbled streets zig-zagging between ancient rustic houses. At the summit is a medieval castle, and although the village has been extensively restored, it has been done with care and sensitivity. There are a number of craft workshops, galleries and a restaurant in the village.

On the coast to the south-east of Thuir is another

enchanting spot, Collioure, without doubt one of the most attractive seaside towns on the Mediterranean. Its charms have been appreciated for a long time and, among many others, Henri Matisse painted here at the beginning of the century. Although nowadays it is thronged with visitors in the summer months, its inherent character and charm seem to have survived almost intact. However, an out-of-season visit is much to be preferred.

The village is situated at the beginning of the coastal *corniche* where the vineyards planted on the steeply plunging slopes are held in place by ancient stone terraces. A cluster of painted fishing boats is pulled up on to the small beach, one side of which is guarded by a small church at the end of a promontory. The Château Royal, once the residence of the kings of Majorca, overlooks the little harbour on the opposite side. The village is famous for its anchovies, and a lively country market is held in the small shaded square on Sunday mornings.

A short distance to the north of the village a narrow country road, the D 86, leads up through the vineyards and into the mountains, through stunning scenery, towards the seventeenth-century chapel of Notre

Above: The fishing village of Collioure. Overleaf: Vineyards near the village of Vingrau.

Dame de Consolation and the Tour Madeloc. As you climb higher, the views, both towards the sea and into the mountains, are simply breath-taking.

Here, on the vertiginous slopes, terraces and drainage ditches originally installed by the Knights Templars enable the vineyards to cover every useful piece of terrain. At the *table d'Orientation* about midway along the route between Collioure and Banyuls-sur-Mer there is a magnificent panoramic view reaching from Narbonne-Plage in the north to Cerbère and Spain in the south. The view is even more spectacular from the Tour Madeloc, which can be reached, preferably on foot, by a very narrow and near perpendicular road. The route returns to the coastal road at Banyuls-sur-Mer.

CÔTES CATALANES

Baixas is a captivating small town situated 10 kilometres or so to the north-west of Perpignan. Surrounded by ramparts and entered by fortified gateways, the town has numerous old houses lining its narrow streets and a church with an extremely beautiful gilded altarpiece dating from the seventeenth century.

On the outskirts of the town is a modern and progressive Cave Co-opérative producing AOC Côtes du Roussillon Villages, Rivesaltes, Muscat de Rivesaltes and Vin de Pays des Côtes Catalanes. It serves a vineyard area of over 2,000 hectares, of which nearly 30% is used to produce Vin de Pays. The *cave* produces a varietal red wine, 'Grenat Catalan', made from Carignan, as well as a blended red, 'Le Pot Dom Brial,' from Merlot, Syrah, Carignan and Grenache, and a white wine from 100% Maccabeo.

The co-operative at Millas on the banks of the Têt, a short distance to the south-west of Baixas, makes a red wine from 100% Merlot, a varietal rosé from Syrah, and a white from Maccebeo with an addition of 10% Grenache Blanc.

There is a tendency for the co-operatives to favour the more traditional local varieties, and for the independent producers to opt for the classic varieties. A good example of the latter is an excellent Chardonnay with the Côtes Catalanes label made by the Domaine Cazes at neighbouring Rivesaltes, a few kilometres to the north-east of Baixas.

From here a short excursion to the north will bring you to the Fort de Salses, a remarkable fifteenth-century fortress built to protect the route which Hannibal took in 218BC, and an outstanding example of military architecture. Built of pinkish stone, with a domed construction, it seems as if it should be guarding an outpost in the Saraha desert.

VALS D'AGLY

From Rivesaltes the D 12 leads north-west into the foothills of the Corbière Mountains passing through spectacular scenery on its way to the wine village of Vingrau, which has a fine thirteenth-century Romanesque church in its centre. Here the local co-operative makes Vin de Pays des Vals d'Agly, a white wine from Maccabeo and Grenache Blanc, and a rosé from a blend of Carignan and Grenache Gris.

The D 9 leads south-west from Vingrau to the nearby wine village of Tautavel. Many important anthropological discoveries have been made in the countryside around the village, the most important being the skull of the Caune de l'Arago man – believed to be more than half a million years old.

Here there is a museum of prehistory as well as the well-respected Cave Co-opérative of the Maître Vignerons de Tautavel. In addition to AOC Côtes du Roussillon Villages, Rivesaltes and Muscat de Rivesaltes, a Muscat Sec is also made with the Vals d'Agly label. M. Mounie, an independent producer, who farms 23 hectares of vines planted near the village, produces a dry but fruity Blanc de Blancs from 100% Maccabeo.

Continuing from Tautavel on the D 9, one can join the main D 117 road to the west of Estagel. This is the birthplace of Dominique François, the nineteenth century astronomer and physicist who is honoured with a monument in the square. The town also possesses a museum of Catalan history.

The co-operative here produces an interesting red Vin de Pays des Côtes Catalanes called 'Grain de Beauté', which is made from a blend of Grenache, Merlot, Syrah and Chenançon. The last is a relatively new variety which has been developed by crossing Grenache Noir with Jurançon, and is beginning to be planted quite widely in the region.

To the south of Estagel the D 612 leads away from the Agly valley and up into the mountains, to a succession of picturesque wine villages. The scenery is breath-taking, with steep slopes patterned by terraced vineyards, plunging valleys and rocky escarpments covered with the dense green foliage of the *garrigue*. During my visit in late January, the hillsides were brilliant with yellow gorse bloom, and dusted with clouds of candy-floss blossom from the almond trees.

A scenic circuit can be made by following the road to Montner and then, after a few kilometres, forking right to Bélesta. Six kilometres to the south, another right fork leads to the prettily situated village of Mont-alba-le-Château, where there is a small museum of wine. From here, head north again to Cassagnes, where the co-operative produces a white Vals d'Agly from Maccabeo and a rosé from Carignan, Grenache and Cinsaut.

Backtracking from here, and soon taking the turning to the right, you come to the hilltop village of Caramany, perched above the valley of the Agly on an outcrop of rock. The co-operative here is known for its AOC Côtes du Roussillon Villages, but it has recently planted Merlot and Cabernet Sauvignon vines with a view to making varietal Vins de Pays in few years' time. This is just one example of how both co-operatives and independent producers regard the production of Vin de Pays as an important way in which they can widen both the variety and style of their wines beyond the limitations imposed by the Appellation Contrôllée regulations.

From Caramany the road descends into the valley of the Agly and follows it to Ansignan, where the impressive remains of a Roman aqueduct can be seen crossing the valley. It is still in use, helping to irrigate the vineyards. A short distance to the south-west of Ansignan a road leads off to the right to Felluns, Le Vivier and St Martin-de-Fenouillet, where M. Saunat makes an excellent Coteaux de Fenouillèdes Chardonnay, before descending to St Paul-de-Fenouillet.

To the north of St Paul the D 7 heads along the Gorges de Galamus, vast jagged clefts in the rock with sheer cliffs and chasms on either side and the silvery thread of a river visible far below. In the summer there is a *caveau* in the gorges, and you can also visit the tiny hermitage of St Antoine de Galamus tucked into the side of the gorge about half-way down.

You can complete a splendidly scenic round trip by continuing to Cubières-sur-Cinoble and then heading eastwards via Soulatgé and Rouffiac-des-Corbières to Cucugnan. From here the route leads up to the Grau de Maury, at the summit of the ridge, and the spectacularly sited Cathar castle of Quéribus. The views

Above: Terraced vineyards on the steep hillsides between Collioure and Banyuls. Overleaf: The valley of the River Maury seen from the Grau de Maury near the château of Quéribus.

over the Maury valley to the Pyrenean peaks are among the finest in the region. The road descends into the village of Maury, known for its Vin Doux Naturel, and then leads back to St Paul and, a short distance further up the valley, Caudiès-de-Fenouillèdes.

COTEAUX DE FENOUILLÈDES

As a general rule, the Caves Co-opératives tend to favour the traditional grape varieties and styles of wine while the independent producers are more likely to be innovative and experimental. The co-operative at Caudiès-de-Fenouillèdes, with 300 producers farming a total of 600 hectares, is a notable exception, and has produced an interesting selection of wines with the Vin de Pays de Coteaux de Fenouillèdes appellation. Three red *vins de cépage* are produced, from Merlot, Syrah and the new variety, Chenançon, and also a *primeur* from Merlot and Carignan. In addition, varietal rosés are made from Syrah and Grenache, as well a pure Chardonnay.

At the Domaine d'Esperet, an independent producer with 100 hectares near Caudiès, a very good Muscat Sec is made with the Vals d'Agly appellation, as well as a red Pyrénées-Orientales from a blend of Carignan, Cinsaut and Merlot.

GRAPE VARIETIES

Opposite: An experimental method of training and pruning Gamay vines in the Côtes de Forez near the village of Marcilly. Above: Freshly picked Chardonnay grapes ready for the wine press.

WINE CHARACTERISTICS

The quality of a wine, and its appeal, can be measured by the presence and balance of certain basic elements, such as fruit, body, tannin, acidity, sweetness, alcohol and aroma.

A red wine needs tannin, but an excess can make it tough or mouth-puckering to drink, while insufficient tannin can make the wine seem lacking in flavour and character. Many very good red wines have a noticeably tannic taste when young, which mellows and softens with age, ultimately producing a wine with more subtle and complex flavours than one which tastes pleasantly soft and fruity soon after it has been bottled.

A white wine needs a degree of acidity, but an excess will make it seem astringent and sharp on the palate, while insufficient acidity is likely to produce a flat or flabby wine, with little character or depth of flavour.

ALICANTE BOUSCHET

A high-yielding variety grown mainly in southern France. Has strong colour and high alcohol potential, but lacks tannin. Used mainly as an element of blended red wines.

ALIGOTÉ

The inferior alternative to Burgundy's Chardonnay, with a tendency towards high acidity. The traditional ingredient of Kir, an aperitif made by spiking white wine with Crème de Cassis.

ALTESSE

Produces full-bodied white wines with a spicy, aromatic bouquet. Also known as Roussette in the Savoie.

ARAMON

A traditional variety of the Languedoc. Its high yield has earned it a reputation for quantity at the expense of quality. However, as one well-known wine-maker told me, it can produce good wine when driven hard.

AUXERROIS BLANC

A generously-yielding variety with high acidity and alcohol potential, making fresh, dry varietal white wines. Grown quite widely between northern Burgundy and Alsace.

BAROQUE

Grown largely in south-west France, and used to make Tursan white wines and some Vins de Pays Landais. High in alcohol, it produces full-bodied country-style wines.

CABERNET FRANC

Widely grown in Bordeaux, it has a softer taste and a more complex aroma than Cabernet Sauvignon. Commonly used as a component of clarets and also in red wines from the Loire, such as Saumur Champigny.

CABERNET SAUVIGNON

Of all the black grapes from which red wines are produced, Cabernet Sauvignon is, perhaps, the one with the widest international popularity. Thought to be derived from wild vines first grown in the Bordeaux area, it remains the foundation of the red wines of that region.

The small, almost sloe-like, purple berries ripen late and contain generous tannin, due in part to an abundance of pips and a high proportion of pulp to juice when pressed. Although initially harsh or tough in character, this grape makes a wine destined to keep and mature. Its bouquet is one of blackcurrant fruit, and ageing produces a fat buttery taste with masses of body and flavour.

CARIGNAN

Widely planted in southern France, it has a generous yield. Produces good colour, tannin and a high degree of alcohol. Used mainly as an element of blended red wines.

CHARDONNAY

Probably the most popular and widely planted white wine grape in the world. Known in France as the white wine grape from which the classic Burgundies, such as Montrachet and Chablis, are made. It is also the grape from which Blanc de Blancs champagne is made. Produces a delicately flavoured, full-bodied wine with a good balance of acidity and alcohol, together with a fragrant aroma. Also has great potential to improve with maturity and lends itself well to oak ageing.

CHASSELAS

A very ancient variety planted largely in the Savoie and Alsace. Produces a light, dry white wine with a tendency towards low acidity and alcohol potential. Also grown as a dessert grape, particularly in Quercy.

CHENIN BLANC

Grown widely in the Loire valley, where it is used to make wines such as Vouvray and Coteaux de Layon. Found less frequently in other parts of France. Also known as Pineau de la Loire.

A high-yielding grape, it produces sweet, honeyed wines and bone dry wines with equal success. Its bouquet is often compared to citrus fruits such as quince and lime, with hints of honey. Also used to make sparkling wines.

CINSAUT

One of the most widely planted varieties in France, where it flourishes in the more southerly climates. Has good acidity and colour and is used often as a blend with Grenache and Carignan, as well as producing varietal red wines.

CLAIRETTE BLANC

Widely planted in southern France, this variety was traditionally used for the production of Vermouth. With a tendency towards low acidity, a fruity bouquet and a high alcohol potential, it is often used as an element in blended Vins de Pays and is sometimes encountered as a varietal white wine.

COLOMBARD

This is the grape from which much of the Armagnac production is distilled. Grown mainly in south-west France, it is used both as an element of blended whites and *vins de cépage*. Makes light, fresh fruity wines with a good bouquet and balance, but best drunk young.

COT

Also known as Malbec or Auxerrois, this variety is grown largely in south-west France and the Midi. Produces soft, easy-to-drink and flavourful red wines. It has relatively low acidity and a flavour which some link with ripe blackberries.

FER SERVADOU

A red wine grape grown largely in the Midi. Used as an element in blended wines such as Madiran and Gaillac.

FOLLE BLANCHE

Grown originally to make brandy, this variety is now found largely in the western Loire, where it is the main ingredient of Gros Plant Nantais. Produces a light, dry wine with little body and a tendency towards high acidity.

GAMAY

The Gamay not only reigns supreme in the Beaujolais but also accounts for a high proportion of French red wines generally. Characteristic of the young fresh fruity reds which constitute the great fount of everyday wine. Produces a light purple-tinged red wine which has good fruit, acidity and bouquet, but is relatively low in tannin and best drunk young. Has a high yield and lends itself well to rapid vinification, making it a popular choice for *primeurs*.

GEWÜRZTRAMINER

Found mainly in north-east France, where it is used to produce varietal dry white wines with a golden tint, high alcohol content, distinctive spicy aroma and complex flavour.

GRENACHE NOIR

Widely planted in southern France, it produces full-bodied fruity rosés as well as dry and quite tough reds. Most commonly used as an element of blended wines, but also encountered as a *vin de cépage*. Blanc and Gris versions of Grenache are also used occasionally in the Languedoc for making white and rosé wines.

Harvesting the grapes on the slopes below the hill village of Offlanges in Franche-Comté.

GROLLEAU

A high-yielding variety, planted largely in the Loire region. Often used to produce a light, fresh-tasting Vin Gris, and also as a component of blended red wines.

JACQUÈRE

A high-yielding variety producing light, dry white wines with relatively high acidity. Planted largely in the Savoie.

JURANÇON

A black grape variety grown largely in south-west France and the Midi, and a relative of the Languedoc's Aramon variety. It produces wine with a relatively high alcohol level and is used primarily as part of a blend.

LEN DE L'ELH

The name derives from *loin de l'oeil*, meaning literally – and inexplicably – far from the eye. A mainstay of the Gaillac region and the Côtes du Tarn, producing a white wine with high alcohol potential but low acidity. Often used in a blend with Mauzac.

MACABEO

A white grape used principally in the most southerly part of Languedoc-Roussillon, to make a fruity, aromatic white wine which is usually quite light and dry. Also known as Maccabeu, it is often used to make white Rioja.

MARSANNE

A high-yielding variety, widely planted in the northern Rhône valley. Produces a honey-coloured white wine with a good bouquet, best drunk young.

MAUZAC BLANC

Planted largely in the Gaillac and Limoux regions. Produces a dry white wine with good fruit and quite high acidity. Also used for sparkling wines, e.g. Blanquette de Limoux, when it is blended with Sauvignon Blanc or Chardonnay. Also known as Blanquette, because of the white powder which coats the undersides of its leaves.

MELON DE BOURGOGNE

Also known as Muscadet in France and Pinot Blanc in California, this grape produces a very dry white wine which can be quite fruity but has a tendency towards high acidity. Popular as a companion to shellfish, and best drunk young.

Spring flowers blooming among the vines near Fleury in the *département* of Aude.

MERLOT

An important high-yield variety grown extensively in south-west France, where it is used as an element of the blend for clarets. It has grown enormously in popularity throughout southern France and is often used to make *vins de cépage*. Valued for its fruitiness and low tannin and acidity, which produce a soft, easy-to-drink red wine.

MONDEUSE NOIRE

Widely planted in north-east France before phylloxera struck. Now found mainly in Savoie and Bugey, it can produce full-bodied, quite tough, varietal red wines with a distinctive character, as well as being used in blended red wines.

MOURVÈDRE

Found in southern France, especially in Provence. Its relatively high acidity, tannin and deep colour are commonly used as a strengthening element in blended reds.

MÜLLER-THURGAU

A German variety, produced by crossing Riesling and Sylvaner. Can produce fragrant white wines which are light, dry and fruity. In France found almost exclusively in Lorraine.

MUSCAT OF ALEXANDRIA

A very ancient, high-yielding variety, used to make both sweet and dry white wines which have a distinctively grapey taste. Requires a hot climate, and is therefore grown largely in southern France. Also planted for dessert grapes.

Muscat Blanc à Petits Grains is a superior variety found in the Roussillon region, where it is used as a component of Vin Doux Naturel such as Banyuls, as well as in the southern Rhône valley for Beaumes de Venise and Clairette de Die.

PINEAU D'AUNIS

Planted largely in the Loire region, this black-skinned variety is often used to make dry, fruity rosé wines. Also used as an element in blended reds.

PINOT NOIR

The great red-wine grape of Burgundy, more fickle and less easily identifiable than the Cabernet Sauvignon. It is grown widely in Alsace, Lorraine, the Savoie and Jura and is an essential ingredient of most champagnes, for which it is pressed swiftly to produce a colourless juice.

A low-yield grape, it produces a wine with flavours of red fruits such as raspberries and plums. Can mature to create highly complex tastes and bouquets, and has an excellent finish and considerable potential to improve with age.

PORTUGAIS BLEU

Grown widely in Germany and Austria, as Portugieser, this red-wine variety is found largely in the Midi. High yielding, with a tendency to low tannin levels, it produces fairly light wines and is used, usually, as an element of a blend.

POULSARD

A black-skinned variety which is planted in eastern France. Produces a light red wine with an attractive, flowery bouquet.

RIESLING

A high-yielding grape which originated in Germany along the banks of the Rhine. Widely grown in north-east France, it is less frequently encountered elsewhere in the country. Susceptible, when harvested late, to *botrytis cinerea*, or noble rot, enabling both sweet and dry wines to be made. With a good balance of acidity and alcohol, it makes wines which are aromatic, fresh and clean tasting with considerable potential to improve with age.

ROUSSANNE

A white wine variety grown largely in the northern Rhône valley. Produces a delicately flavoured white wine with a scented bouquet, and is used both as an element of a blended wine, often with Marsanne, and for *vins de cépage*.

SAUVIGNON BLANC

This grape produces the great French white wines of Sancerre and Pouilly-Fumé. Also an important element in

Aramon vines over 100 years old in the Coteaux de Salavès near the village of Durfort.

the white wines of Graves, blended with Semillon. Widely grown in many other regions of France, where it has become a popular choice for varietal Vins de Pays. Produces a light, fresh wine with a hint of green fruit in the bouquet and a flinty-dry flavour, but has a limited potential to improve with keeping.

SEMILLON

Widely grown in south-west France, the Semillon grape is used as a component of dry white wines, often in combination with Sauvignon Blanc. Like the Riesling it is also ideal for the generation of noble rot, when a highly concentrated juice is pressed to make sweet white wines like Sauternes. Produces a strongly alcoholic wine, relatively low in acidity, with a limited bouquet and what is usually described as a grassy, lemony flavour.

SYRAH

The grape from which many of the red Rhône wines, such as Hermitage, derive their great strength and character. It survives well on poor soil, produces a good yield and has an abundance of tannin, making strongly alcoholic wines with plenty of body

and flavour which have the potential for high quality and improvement with keeping. Now also popular for varietal Vin de Pays rosés.

TANNAT

A variety used to make Madiran, one of the most interesting wines of south-west France, as well as red Côtes de St Mont. Strong in colour, tannin and alcohol, it has a perfumed bouquet and benefits from ageing.

TERRET BOURRET

Planted widely in the Languedoc coastal region. Gris grapes are grown as well as white, producing light, dry white wines with good acidity.

TERRET NOIR

A variety grown largely in southern France, producing a light red wine with a pleasing bouquet and some acidity. Used mainly as part of a blend.

TIBOUREN

A black grape grown mainly in southern France, notably Provence. Lends itself well to making full-bodied rosés with a distinctive bouquet.

UGNI BLANC

This high-yielding grape is responsible for producing more white wine world-wide than any other variety. In France a large proportion is distilled into brandy. It has a limited bouquet, high acidity and little body. Often used as an acidic element of a blend, but sometimes found as a *vin de cépage*. Also known as Italy's Trebbiano and Cognac's St Emilion.

VIOGNIER

A variety associated primarily with the northern Rhône valley, but becoming increasingly popular for Vins de Pays throughout southern France, albeit in small plantings. Produces a full-bodied white wine with a very distinctive, aromatic bouquet, and is nearly always used to produce *vins de cépage*.

INDEX